# JETLINER CABINS

**Jennifer Coutts Clay**

**WILEY-ACADEMY**

## Acknowledgements

Parts of this book are based on a series of articles that I wrote for *Aircraft Interiors* magazine, from 2000 to 2002. I would like to thank Mr Azin Hatefi, Editor and Publisher, and his team, headquartered in California, for their professional advice. It has been an honour to serve on their Advisory Panel.

I am grateful to the manufacturers, airlines, suppliers and vendors who have supported the project. I would also like to thank my family members and friends, who encouraged me to develop the concepts; my colleagues and the specialists, whose valuable suggestions, quotations and pictures helped bring my text to life; Mr Larry Stockel for his work on graphics; Ms Carol Anderson, Mr Andrew Boynton and Ms Kate Norris for their expert handling of the material during the process of compilation; and the systems department and Ms Robin Verdino at Clay Finlay, Inc for improving my information-technology programmes.

Special thanks go to Mr Gerry Draper who, at British Airways in the 1970s, introduced a generation of aviation devotees, including this writer, to the challenges of airline product marketing and customer service.

In memory of my parents, a portion of the revenues from the sale of this work will be donated to the Royal Air Force Benevolent Fund.

Finally, my thanks are due to Ms Abigail Grater and Ms Mariangela Palazzi-Williams for the help and guidance they have provided throughout this project; and to Mr Mario Bettella for his inspired handling of the intricacies of the design of this book.

**Photocredits**: Grateful acknowledgement is given to the airlines and other organizations credited in this book for permission to use their photographs. All other pictures are from the collection of J Clay Consulting

*Front cover: Computer-simulated aircraft-interior design scheme, Courtesy Computergraphics ACA and Lantal Textiles*

# Contents

Introduction                                      4

## Product Branding                               10

Chapter  1   First-Class Luxury                   12
Chapter  2   Business-Class Comfort               26
Chapter  3   Economy-Class Value                  40
Chapter  4   Aero Identity                        50

## Passenger Experience                           60

Chapter  5   Sky Lights                           62
Chapter  6   Dining à la Jet Set                  70
Chapter  7   Real-Feel Customer Touchpoints       78
Chapter  8   Accessibility: Special Needs         90

## Cabin Maintenance                              100

Chapter  9   Look Smart: Keep Clean               102
Chapter 10   Durability                           114
Chapter 11   Magic Carpet                         122
Chapter 12   The Leather Forecast                 130

## Marketing Challenge                            140

Chapter 13   Flying Colours                       142
Chapter 14   Concorde Unique                      152
Chapter 15   Upgrades: Refurbishing Aloft         164
Chapter 16   Ways Ahead                           176

Bibliography                                      185
Directory of Specialists                          186
Airline Websites                                  189
Index                                             190

4

# INTRODUCTION

*To: The Wright Brothers*
*Kitty Hawk, North Carolina*

Dear Wilbur and Orville,

This year is the centenary of your great achievement – the first powered, sustained and controlled flight. The actual date of the celebrations will be 17 December, but *Jetliner Cabins* is taking this opportunity to offer early congratulations. (Some people might complain that the Wright Flyer of 1903 did not have a cabin, but we ignore such cavils.)

The prehistory of aviation is filled with examples of wild optimism, and many of the plans drawn up by would-be aviators, for others to test-fly, demonstrate that imagination was certainly not in short supply. For example, a most intriguing proposal was that if a sufficiently large flock of geese were harnessed together they could pull a chariot through the sky.

However, the journey to powered flight actually began in Switzerland in 1738 when Daniel Bernoulli, the greatest among an entire family of geniuses, promulgated the Bernoulli theorem that 'An increase in fluid velocity is associated with a decline in fluid pressure', and in fact this is all we need to know in order to make an aircraft fly. In specific aviation terms, if the air flowing over the top of the wings is travelling faster than the air underneath them, the air pressure on top will be lower than the pressure below and the difference will pull everything up. This phenomenon is called 'lift', and it beats a flock of geese any day!

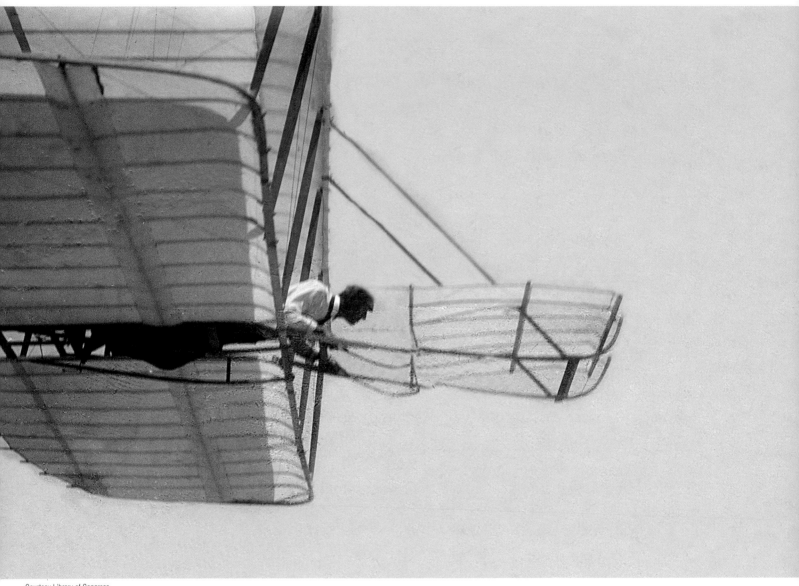

Courtesy Library of Congress

Bernoulli had solved the problem of lift, but that of 'control' remained intractable and optimists continued to dive assorted contraptions into the unforgiving earth or, sometimes, the sea. The German Otto Lilienthal was the first to fly gliders that could land in one piece with some consistency, and he made more than two thousand flights before his untimely death in 1896.

You learned from him, and added yet more experience – another one thousand glides – though experience in these new skills was not easily or cheaply bought. Your reward for many years of effort came on 17 December 1903, and although the five spectators present at this great moment in history were widely disbelieved when they claimed to have seen a man fly, the world was convinced by further demonstrations that the impossible had actually occurred.

Perhaps the most striking of all the circumstances of your achievement was that the prize was won not by giant companies with huge research budgets or by rich individuals in search of excitement, but by two brothers from a modest background, working with their own hands in their own bicycle shop. This, it was sometimes said, was the event that introduced the 'Century of the Common Man'. So, in a sense, it was. But in many other ways you were very uncommon men. You opened the era of aviation.

Your successes inspired generations of intrepid aviators to pursue their aerial passions. Memorable names from the history books include Alcock, Blériot, Breguet, Brown, Curtiss, Earhart, Fokker, Johnson, Kingsford-Smith, Lindbergh, Markham, Saint-Exupéry, Santos-Dumont, Sikorsky and von Zeppelin. They, and other legendary aviation pioneers, made the marvel of flight a reality in even the most remote parts of the world, and it was their sense of mission that eventually led to the creation of the mass transportation systems that are now an everyday feature of modern life.

Courtesy Library of Congress

Courtesy Library of Congress

The aim of *Jetliner Cabins* is to survey just one small part of the vast legacy that we have inherited from you: the development of the commercial-aircraft cabin environment from the late 1970s to the turn of the millennium. Main topics include product branding, the passenger experience, cabin maintenance and the marketing challenge, and include comments from more than forty international specialists in the field.

Wilbur and Orville, it has been both a privilege and a pleasure to create this work. We salute you, and look forward to seeing you, in spirit at least, at Kitty Hawk, North Carolina, in December.

Yours sincerely,

Jennifer Coutts Clay

www.jclayconsulting.com

New York

Courtesy Library of Congress

Product Branding

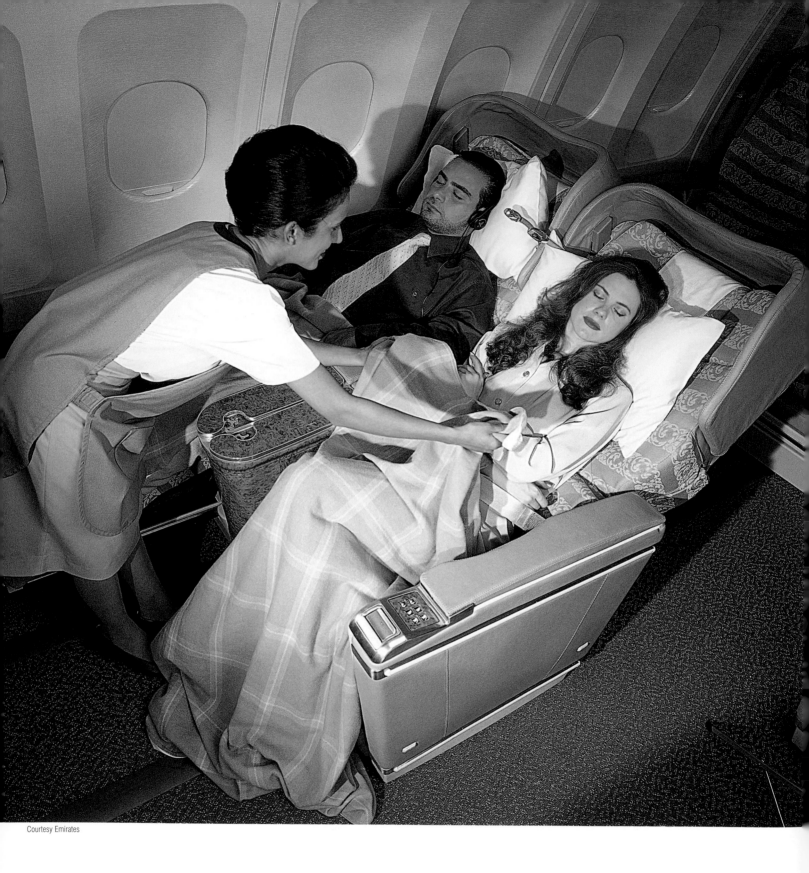

12

# Chapter 1
## FIRST-CLASS LUXURY

*How much does it cost? On the New York–London route, at the turn of the millennium, the first-class round trip published fare was around US$10,000. What can these passengers expect for their money? And how does it feel to fly in the first-class salons in the sky?*

When customers buy first-class tickets they expect the ultimate in *luxury* from the airline they choose. In the first-class cabin they assume that they will experience superlative style, service and comfort. As a result the airlines, in their battle to win the continued allegiance of high-paying customers, have to constantly upgrade their product standards.

In recent years there have been many welcome developments:

- cabin environments that are lighter, fresher and more gracious;
- more spacious passenger-seating areas;
- the installation of 'furniture' that is both useful and elegant; for example, work tables, bars, consoles and sideboards;
- in-flight entertainment systems that are more versatile;
- galleys that are more efficient and offer healthier food-and-beverage choices;
- larger coat closets;
- dressing rooms;
- larger lavatories (now called bathrooms), some with windows;
- an increase in stowage options for passengers' carry-on articles; and
- an ever-growing range of high-tech options for users of telephones, fax machines and computers.

Not surprisingly, given that passengers typically spend about 95 per cent of their time on board the aircraft sitting in their assigned seats, one of the keys to 'retained preference' is the aircraft seat itself. And in the past 20 years there has been steady progress toward ever-higher standards of safety, security and comfort in this area. Traditionally major airlines offered an ingenious assortment of portable ottomans and footstools. During the 1980s, however, on their long-haul routes Pan Am and TWA pioneered the introduction of extendable legrests that enabled customers to keep their legs at a comfortable height and angle throughout the flight. The pull-out structures – made principally of metal tubing – were lightweight and relatively easy to deploy, and could just as easily fold or collapse when a neighbouring passenger brushed past or if the aircraft encountered turbulence.

### SWEET DREAMS

These flimsy 'deck chair' constructions were eventually superseded by electrically operated padded legrest panels similar to those used on dentists' chairs. When passengers pulled the correct levers, or pushed the appropriate combination of buttons, the upholstered panels would extend from below the individual seat cushions. To enable passengers to sleep comfortably, however, it was also necessary to provide a greater degree of seat-back recline. Stage by stage, by removing individual seats or entire

Courtesy Emirates

Courtesy Pan Am/George Design Studio

At the beginning of the 1980s in the first-class cabins of the major airlines, the extendable footrest, as developed by Pan Am (above), was regarded as a luxurious accessory. By the end of the millennium, passengers could expect to stretch out and snooze on full-length sleeper seats or beds (as shown in this Chapter)

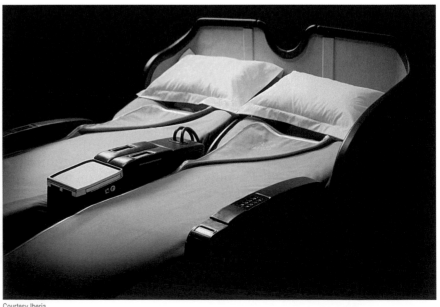

Courtesy Iberia

rows, the leading airlines increased the proportion of open space in their first-class cabins, and added new features including:

- more turnaround space for passengers to get to and from the window seats without disturbing the passengers in the adjoining aisle seats;
- extra stowage compartments, to give passengers easy access to their belongings;
- wider armrests, padded for comfort;
- contoured support in the headrest area at the top of the seat back;
- pivoting meal tray-tables;
- slide-out cocktail trays;
- individual reading lights;
- pull-out coat hooks; and
- pull-down holders for beverage containers.

However, in 1995 there was a great leap forward when British Airways launched a dramatically new first-class cabin programme. As part of a US$800-million product-improvement plan, the airline announced the complete redesign of the first-class section of its long-haul, wide-body, twin-aisle fleet. This was the equivalent of a quantum leap in the aviation business: from then on, all carriers offering full first-class service had to take into account the new design concepts that would rapidly become a benchmark for the entire industry.

The programme was initially launched to help the airline gain supremacy on the North Atlantic routes; 35 per cent of all air travel is between North America and Europe, and this is regarded as the toughest battleground in the aviation world. Of a number of market-research programmes, one in particular had indicated that more than 80 per cent of first-class passengers were travelling

Courtesy Qantas

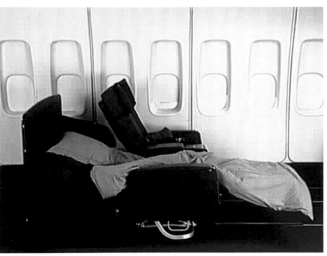

Courtesy Air France

Courtesy Air France

*1995 was a good year for exciting new aviation design programmes. Introduced into service in early summer, the Air France first-class, lie-flat sleeper seat was hailed as a revolutionary advance because it provided new standards of spaciousness and comfort.*

alone, and based on this the central feature of the new pro-gramme was the introduction of the individual 'pod'. A semi-enclosed compartment, set at an angle, facing toward the side of the aircraft, this offered high-revenue customers much greater privacy and comfort than had existed with the old-style conventional sleeper seats, which had been arranged in straight rows, as in a classroom, and also reduced to near zero the amount of disconcerting eye contact, passenger to passenger as well as passenger to flight attendant.

Other features of the pod included:
- a table;
- a visitor's seat;
- an individual gooseneck reading light;
- a personal TV-and-video entertainment system; and
- a telephone.

The first-class cabin of a Boeing B747 has 14 pods, compared with 18 sleeper seats in the airline's previous configuration. Four of the pods are situated in two sets of two, in the centre of the cabin, so that two passengers can travel next to each other. However, if these passengers want privacy, they can activate a special privacy screen between the two seats. The armchair within the pod can be converted into a flat bed measuring 78 inches (1.98 metres), sufficient for a tall person plus 'wriggle room'. When passengers wish to sleep, the flight attendants make up the beds using crisp linen sheets, pillows and duvet-style quilts. Passengers are also offered sporting-style sleeping suits.

The new approach to the layout of the British Airways first-class cabin was actually derived from the world of luxury yacht interiors. In keeping with this maritime heritage, the pod compartments were given wood-effect panelling on the upper section of the shell surrounds, while the lower section trim features a soft, light blue suede-finish fabric.

Courtesy British Airways

Launched to great acclaim by British Airways in September 1995, this semi-enclosed, individual compartment 're-benchmarked' first-class travel (as explained in this Chapter). Designed as an ultra-luxurious efficiency centre, this model of practicability has to provide living space, sleeping accommodation, dining, work and entertainment facilities while at the same time complying with all mandated safety certification requirements (as described in Chapter 15/ Upgrades: Refurbishing Aloft)

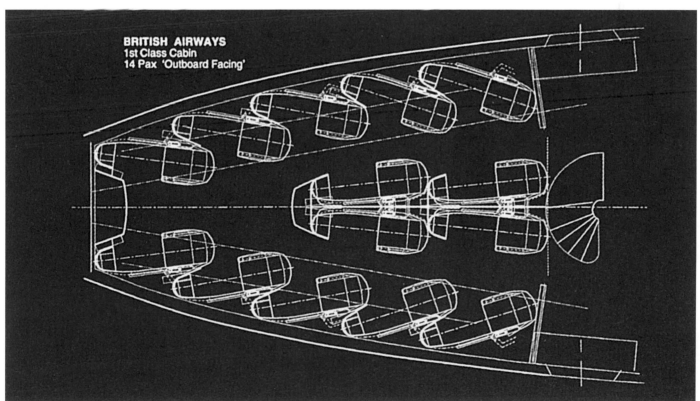

Courtesy British Airways

Courtesy Lufthansa

*The unusual, corrugated-metal-look treatment on the side panels of this Lufthansa first-class sleeper seat has historically interesting connotations (as described in this Chapter)*

Courtesy Qantas

In addition, the meal service was changed to individual à la carte service; that is, individual passengers can eat whenever they want. The traditional trolley service, whereby passengers were served meals communally, was no longer possible because the shape of the aisles had been changed. Consequently, individual passenger meals are now served, for the most part, 'pre-plated'.

This breakthrough first-class product was launched around the same time that British Airways was implementing its highly controversial Worldwide Art Programme, in which individual, unusual decorative treatments were applied to the tail fins of each aircraft. The corporate departure from the traditional national flag treatment generated an incredible amount of attention among the flying, and the non-flying, public, both at home and abroad. Almost every press report that lambasted the 'weird, ethnic tails' had something positive to say about the marvellous new 'super-cocoons', or 'wonder-beds', that were now tucked into the nose of the aircraft, and thus the pods benefited enormously from the controversy.

However, on further examination the British Airways pod was not quite as radical or innovative as travellers and the press might have imagined. During the mid-1990s, as new, powerful aircraft started to fly non-stop over greater distances, a number of long-haul carriers moved to upgrade the service standards in their first- and business-class cabins – after all, some 40 per cent or even more of their revenue can come from their premium passengers.

Early in 1995, Air France had pioneered an innovative new product, L'Espace, described as 'the future of airline travel'. The spend was US$100 million on large first-class sleeper seats that recline to a full 180 degrees, transforming into horizontal 'beds' that are 77 inches (1.96 metres) long. Each seat position has a vertical privacy divider at the headrest area, plus a personal TV-and-video set and a telephone. The new-style cabin was configured in the traditional straight rows, and 13 sleeper seats were installed in the 'A' zone (the nose section) of a Boeing B747. The aisle layout was left unchanged, so meals can be served to passengers as a group, using the normal trolley routine.

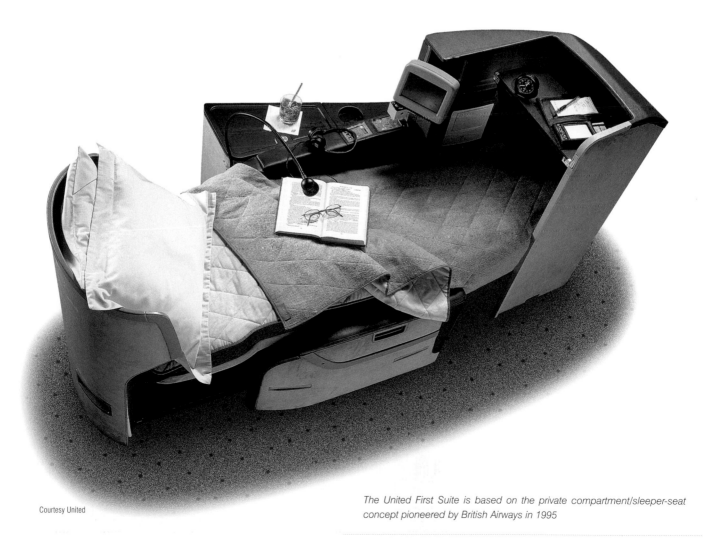

Courtesy United

*The United First Suite is based on the private compartment/sleeper-seat concept pioneered by British Airways in 1995*

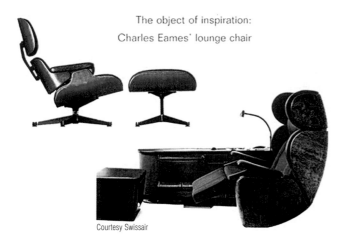

The object of inspiration:
Charles Eames' lounge chair

Courtesy Swissair

*The rounded contours of the Swissair first-class sleeper seat (above), introduced into service at the turn of the millennium, derive from the Charles Eames Lounge Chair which dates from the 1940s and 1950s*

*The seating layout of this Qantas first-class cabin (right) is similar to the configuration pioneered by British Airways (as shown in the diagram earlier in this Chapter)*

Courtesy Qantas

Also, in 1994, prior to the Air France upgrade, Airbus had produced some daringly innovative designs for the first-class cabin of *its* long-haul, wide-body, twin-aisle aircraft. Thomas Bock, Director of Advanced Design at Airbus, explains: 'The company's proposals for a programme with Qantas were presented in computer graphic format and, adorned with happy kangaroos on floors and walls, showed concepts for a 1+2+1 seating layout: along the sidewalls of the cabin, there are single seats; in the middle of the cabin, there are double seats. Each seat is next to an aisle and has an individual canopy hood for privacy. The sidewall seats can turn or "swivel", to form small outboard dining groups. The centre seats can also swivel, thus providing the option of having a large, communal dining- or work table in the central area of the cabin.'

**FLIGHT TO QUALITY**
During the late 1990s, as a consequence of developing trends in

improved service standards and changes in regulatory requirements (see Chapter 15/Upgrades: Refurbishing Aloft), all long-haul airlines were forced to reconsider their position in the first-class market. Some dropped first class and moved to a two-class service instead. Others, however, decided to put money, time and effort into upgrading their first-class cabins.

Lufthansa, for example, developed a distinctive presentation: seat covers in deep blue, plus a corrugated-metal-look decorative treatment on the seat side panels derived from the exterior contouring of the famous Junkers, the world's first all-metal aircraft. And Singapore Airlines inaugurated an elegant first-class cabin scheme, the aesthetic approach of which derived from luxury rail-car interiors – an unusual combination of leather, suede and wood-look treatments, in natural colours. The 14-inch (35.56-centimetre) video monitor at each lie-flat sleeper-seat position was the largest of its kind at the time. The installation of a stationery drawer in the

Courtesy Japan Airlines

Courtesy Swissair

stylish table/work desk, provided a welcome solution to the perennial problem of where to store all those things such as reading glasses, notebooks, eye masks and so on during the flight. United and Qantas followed the lead set by British Airways and installed first-class pod compartments.

American Airlines launched the Flagship Suite, featuring exclusive swivel seats with lumbar support. The seat width is 21 inches (53.34 centimetres), becoming 30.5 inches (77.47 centimetres) when both armrests are dropped. Configured in the bed position, the length is 78 inches (1.98 metres). The rounded cubicle structure is comfortably roomy, and recessed into the rear-facing exterior shell at floor level are latched storage lockers – a safe haven for shoes, purses and valuables.

In the Far East, Japan Airlines, Thai International Airways and Asiana installed 'headboxes' to provide privacy for sleeping first-class passengers. Although the appearance of some of the

Courtesy Philippine Airlines

*In the mid-1980s first-class passengers on Philippine Airlines could sleep through overnight flights in these upper- and lower-level bunk beds*

early models was rather basic, passengers found that the partitioning worked in an efficient way, successfully blocking out noise and disturbance.

Then, just when it seemed that the world's major airlines had reached a level of perfection in the first-class cabin, along came something else. Only four years after the launch of the British Airways pod compartments, Swissair (the forerunner of Swiss International Air Lines) announced the development of a completely new first-class seat: the Eames 'Chair-in-the-Air'.

It should be remembered that for centuries chairs were constructed like boxes. Even today the Queen, when she opens Parliament, sits on a platform-type throne that consists of flat surfaces and 90-degree angles – as indeed has almost every monarch throughout recorded history. The Eames chair, by contrast, dating from the 1940s and 1950s in America, was the first to be designed around the contours of the human body – that is, around compound curves. Bringing this concept into the aircraft-cabin environment was an enormous challenge technically, but the results were instantaneous: passengers immediately reported that they loved the comfort and solidity of this new, large, rounded style of seat that flies now on Swiss International Air Lines. The design was subsequently adopted by South African Airways (see Chapter 4/Aero Identity). In the post-Second World War era, Mr and Mrs Eames stated – in the soundest capitalist terms – that their mission was to deliver 'the most of the best to the greatest number of people for the least'. Could they in their wildest dreams have imagined then that their unique approach would, half a century later, be implemented inside jetliner cabins?

With new aircraft types offering flights of ever greater duration, all long-haul carriers now have to battle to stay competitive in the sleeper-seat market. The forthcoming Airbus A380 will offer several options, including the possibility of installing bunk beds in the lower-lobe section of the aircraft; these could be converted into tables to enable the sleeping compartment to function as a meeting room. In the mock-up models of the aircraft, it is possible to stand up straight, turn around and stretch without feeling constrained in any way. However, because there are no windows on the lower deck, it is possible that some passengers may feel claustrophobic, and it might therefore be appropriate to consider using this special part of the aircraft for sleeping accommodation. But – and here is the marketing dilemma – should passengers be given a bed and a seat for one fare? Or should they be asked to pay extra for both a bed and a seat? The difficulty of handling competitive fare levels could create make-or-break scenarios for individual airline operators in the years to come. However, the predictions from the specialist manufacturers show that pods are here to stay, for both the foreseeable and the longer-term future.

Although the sleeper seat was trumpeted as the great product innovation of the first-class cabin during the 1990s, there were in fact a number of honourable precedents, including the luxurious bunk beds that flew on Philippine Airlines during the 1980s. These were unique in that they were certified for use during both takeoff and landing. And, because they were located longitudinally on the upper deck of the Boeing B747 – where there are lots of windows – passengers could enjoy, in total luxury, a bird's-eye view of the passing clouds.

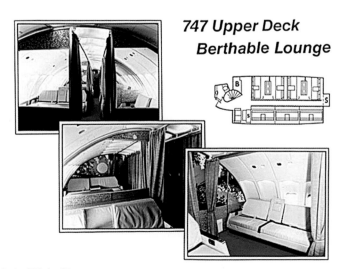

## 747 Upper Deck
## Berthable Lounge

*On a long flight, what could be more luxurious than to socialise and relax in this 'Berthable Lounge'? At night, the sofas could be used as bunk beds*

Courtesy Philippine Airlines

Courtesy Airbus/Thomas Bock

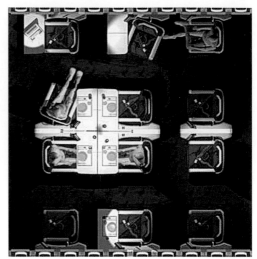

Courtesy Airbus/Thomas Bock

*These computer graphics date from early 1994. Formulated for presentation to prospective customers, they show dramatically new proposals for the first-class cabins of the wide-body aircraft then being built by Airbus (details are provided earlier in this Chapter)*

## COMMENTS FROM THE SPECIALISTS

### Barbara Bermack
*Travel Consultant, Mercury International Travel, New York*
Those who fly first class are cosseted, coddled and catered to. No one enjoys better service, and no passenger is more coveted by the airlines. These are the clients who are the most discerning travellers in the world, and they expect nothing but the best. Leisure travellers will save up their frequent-flyer miles for years to be able to trade them in for first-class tickets, and business travellers usually have to attain the very top two or three positions in their companies to be able to fly first class with any consistency.

What started on a grand scale with British Airways sleeper seats has now blossomed into an era in which all other carriers have to measure up or lose revenue. I have clients who will jump carriers if one offers a sleeper seat on a desired route and another does not. On long-haul flights, such as from the US to the Far East, or from Europe to Asia or Africa, it's become mandatory for first-class cabins to be redesigned to incorporate all these new amenities. Power-supply outlets, meals on demand, varied choices of in-flight entertainment, private meeting space and exceptional service have become the standard. But as airlines struggle to capture market share they are being forced to come up with ever-expanding and innovative ideas.

New ideas being tossed around sound like a science-fiction film. Among these are dry-cleaning services, on-board showers, staffed business centres for long haul flights, and even a first-class apartment with a queen- or king-size bed. One really has to wonder when the sublime will finally become the ridiculous. Stay tuned. Nothing in this industry surprises me anymore.

### Michael M Boland
*President and CEO, Maritz Travel Company, Chesterfield, Missouri*
Some first-class cabins are truly special – sleeper beds with fresh sheets and pajamas, widely varied meals on demand, fine wines and flight attendants who call you by name. This emerging focus on the aircraft interior environment is not balanced by the service on the ground. The lack of space, care or priority for first-class passengers often offsets the fine on-board experience. The boarding process, for example, often means simply being at the front of the herd.

It's also interesting to note that as first class has become more elaborate fewer of the passengers in the first-class cabin are full-fare-paying customers. Frequent-flyer upgrades have made their way into these cabins.

### Phyllis Martin-Vegue
*Principal, and Director, Interiors Studio, SMWM, San Francisco, California*
These comments describe our work for American Airlines at the time of the development of the international first-class Flagship Suite for the Boeing B777.

In the late 1990s, as American began the largest fleet refurbishment programme in its history, it conducted extensive research to understand the trends in first-class travel at the beginning of the twenty-first century. The airline consulted with its *frequent* customers by means of focus groups, questionnaires, full-scale mock-ups and test flights to determine customer preferences. These continuing sessions informed the comfort and design levels that would satisfy and please American's *loyal* customers.

It was determined at the outset that the overall approach to the interior of the aircraft cabin was to be holistic; that is, treated as a complete environment, one in which issues of scale, modelling, form, volume, lighting, colours, patterns, textures and details mattered more than they had in the past.

The airline established that there would be strong appeal to its loyal customers in a seat that would allow convivial seating arrangements, while providing each passenger with a privacy option. American Airlines theorized that there would also be marketable appeal to passengers from other cultures to choose this service when looking for a typically 'American' experience. This was a different philosophy from that associated with the individual pod-style compartments developed by British Airways.

Working with SMWM, its overall cabin- and seat-styling design firm, American directed the development of the first commercially approved swivel seat, giving its customers the option to dine, conference and converse in comfortable groups *à deux* or in groups of four. The SMWM designers created a sleek design incorporating a curvilinear, sweeping low partition that wraps each seat in a 'private cabin' and allows for a two- to four-person conference or dining option. This partition creates a central 'spine' that runs the length of the first-class cabin and accommodates an integrated console housing all the luxury facilities: touch-deployed in-flight entertainment screen, recessed front table, retractable privacy divider, pocket for laptop storage, power-supply outlet and custom mood-lighting fixture.

*All aviation product prototypes must undergo stringent testing processes in a design mock-up studio. Assessing the comfort levels of a sleeper seat can be an exhausting task, but someone has to do it!*

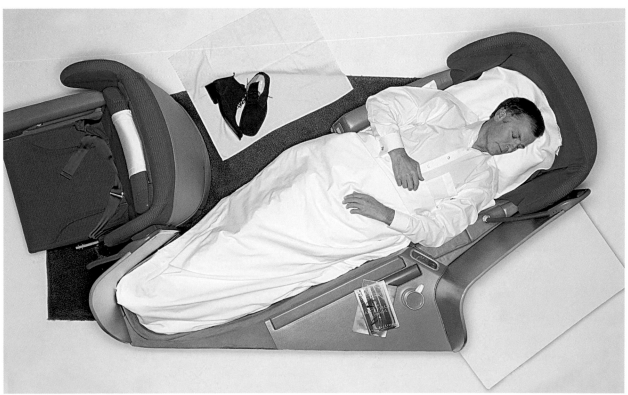

Courtesy British Airways

Courtesy Continental

# Chapter 2
## BUSINESS-CLASS COMFORT

*How much does it cost? On the New York–London route, at the turn of the millennium, the business-class round trip published fare on both a three-class carrier and a two-class carrier was around US$6000. What can these passengers expect for their money? And how does it feel to fly in the business-class salons in the sky?*

When customers buy business-class tickets they expect to be able to travel in *comfort*. In the business-class cabin they want to feel free to manage their flying time effectively, and to do this they require a reasonable amount of space where they can work, sleep, eat and relax.

During the 1980s when the major three-class airlines started to fly dedicated business-class cabins, most carriers opted for six- or seven-abreast seating in the main-deck areas. The aircraft seats were wider than those in economy class, measuring approximately 18 inches (45.72 centimetres) across the seat cushion. The armrests were also 1 inch (2.54 centimetres) or so wider than those in economy class. Over the years, seat pitch (the distance between seat rows, measured from 'like point' to 'like point') gradually increased to between 40 inches (1.06 metres) and 50 inches (1.27 metres), the seats reclined to approximately 130 to 140 degrees, and brochures started to emphasize 'More knee room, greater leg room'.

However, following the product breakthroughs in the first-class market during the 1990s (see Chapter 1/First-Class Luxury), it was inevitable that business class would be affected and that the major airlines would have to adopt a fresh approach to their product positioning. Early in the 1990s, KLM, Northwest and SAS

ceased to offer a dedicated first-class service, and launched new-style 'two-class' operations. Over the course of the decade a hybrid product that blurred the boundaries between the old first-class and business-class cabins evolved in the form of, for example, Premier Class at Aer Lingus, Business First at Continental, Grand Class at Austrian Airlines and Magnifica Class at Alitalia. Seats in these business-class cabins are usually configured 2+2+2 or 2+3+2, so that no one has to step past more than one passenger in order to get to the aisle.

In recent years the two-class carriers have gained in strength, taking advantage of the fact that where cost-cutting is necessary companies have been tending to ban first-class travel privileges for all but their very top executives.

The thinking behind the plans for these new two-class services was based on the model of the first-class product offered by the three-class carriers during the late 1980s and early 1990s. For example, when Continental launched its Business First product in the mid-1990s there were obvious parallels with the first-class sleeper-seat products that were flying on the major carriers at the time. The new Continental sleeper seat had a generous amount of recline, an all-cloth seat cover, an adjustable headrest, and an electronic legrest, footrest and lumbar support. On the airline's

Courtesy Continental

long-haul, wide-body, twin-aisle aircraft, the seat-pitch measurement was 60 inches (1.52 metres), and the seating configuration was 2+2+2. Personal video entertainment systems were built into the armrest consoles, and hot face towels and four- or five-course meals were available. In addition, the airline offered an on-demand meal-option menu selection – passengers could choose to eat what they wanted, when they wanted it. This new approach to space, comfort and service, all at business-class fares, turned out to be one of the great value-for-money product developments for business executives.

Subsequently, more and more airlines took the plunge. In the spring of 1999, Delta dropped its three-class service and moved to two-class, launching its Business Elite cabin, which was deliberately structured to supersede all the main product features of its competition. The airline's mission was to be 'Simply the Best'.

The Delta business-class seat has 11 individual control points:
- six-way headrest adjustment;
- a passenger control pad with a telephone;
- a power-supply outlet for laptop computers;
- a footplate (manually deployed);
- a one-step button for landing preparation that automatically adjusts the seat to the full upright position and stows the legrest;
- seat-back recline;

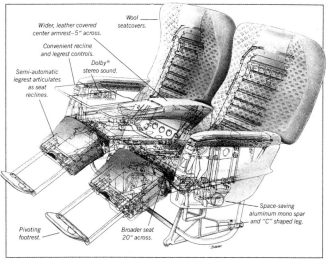

Courtesy TWA

Courtesy Air France

Courtesy Continental

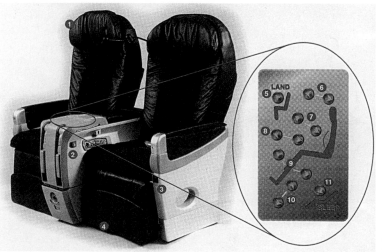

Courtesy Delta Air Lines

*In the mid-1980s TWA introduced a new cradle-type, business-class seat complete with pivoting footrest (see the schematic diagram, above). Over the next 15 years, airlines developed increasingly sophisticated products for their business-class travellers (as shown on this page)*

Courtesy Air France

Courtesy ANA

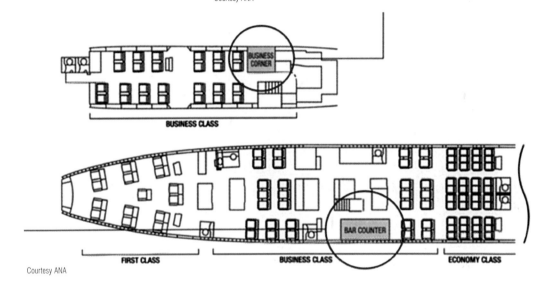

Courtesy ANA

*Aiming at increasing their share of the business-travel market, airlines have installed self-service bars and business work stations on board their aircraft (see also the on-board bars in Chapter 5/Sky Lights, Chapter 10/Durability and Chapter 15/Upgrades: Refurbishing Aloft)*

- lumbar adjustment;
- seat-cushion adjustment;
- legrest adjustment;
- calf-support adjustment;
- a sleep button that automatically adjusts the seat to full recline with a fully extended legrest; and
- individual, in-seat gooseneck reading lights.

The seats are upholstered in a way that is reminiscent of a high-powered executive suite: glossy, navy blue leather-covered seat surrounds and a comfortable fabric-covered central insert panel. An in-seat video screen is located in the centre console, between the seats. The passenger control pad, which is released by pushing a lever, is located in the central armrest panel, also between the seats, and passengers can select from a number of entertainment options, including audio, video, movies and games. The

telephone is activated by sliding a credit card through the card-reader slot.

Delta's new service also offered five-course meals and a special wine service, added features that had previously been associated only with the luxury offerings in the first-class cabins of the three-class carriers.

## CUSTOMER BENEFITS ANALYSIS

In recent years, a number of carriers have added special refinements to their business-class cabins. For example, of the three-class carriers Air France has a high-tech style, eat-when-you-like bar. ANA's Tokyo–Chicago service has a sit-down bar counter located between the first- and business-class cabins, and on the upper deck of the Boeing B747 a business corner offers an on-board fax service and certified-to-fly revolving chairs.

Courtesy Virgin Atlantic

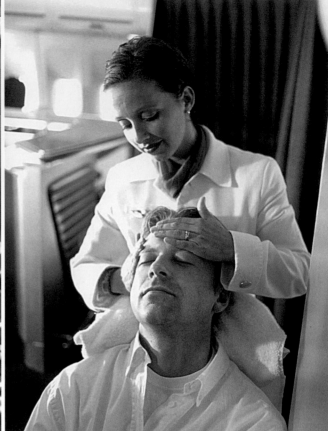

Courtesy Virgin Atlantic

Of the two-class carriers, Virgin Atlantic's Upper Class service includes a custom-designed beauty salon where a beauty thera-pist provides rejuvenating treatments such as:

- 'Stress Busting' – face and scalp massage;
- 'Full Back Up' – to unwind at 30,000 feet;
- 'Helping Hands' – special zone therapy;
- 'Handsome Hands' – personal manicure; and
- 'Armed Force' – 'the ultimate stress-relieving shoulder massage'.

And the airline's central welcome area, which during its early days of operation was a relatively modest knee-level coffee table, has now been transformed into a glamourous, glittering cocktail bar complete with dramatic mood-lighting programmes pioneered by Virgin Atlantic.

During the late 1990s, the two-class carriers aggressively attacked the business market and were successful in diverting a large number of profitable passengers away from the three-class carriers that flew the traditional-style business-class cabins. In an attempt to counter the new competitive forces, a number of three-class carriers installed more modern, ergonomically con-structed 'cradle-type' pivoting seats. Features included movable headrests, air-bag supports for the lower back, and neck supports

Courtesy Virgin Atlantic

31

Courtesy Continental

known as 'Mickey Mouse ears' or 'Mae Wests'. However, these 'flying cradles' were basically armchairs with extendable footrests, and not really stretch-out-and-sleep seats.

Though in some cases the traditional three-class carriers even had to consider lowering fare levels on specific routes, an alternative approach was to meet the competition head-on by installing sleeper seats in business class on designated aircraft units scheduled to fly on those routes where the three-class carrier faced direct competition from the two-class sleeper-seat carriers. However, a decision to 'split the fleet' in this way is never made lightly; even when individual aircraft units are locked into specific routes, it can be extremely difficult to manage a dual approach,

particularly regarding the specialist coverage required in the fields of maintenance and logistics. It can also be a dangerous move, potentially, in that the level of product integrity of the carrier might eventually be compromised, for example at times when it is necessary to substitute one aircraft for another.

**LONG-TERM STRATEGY**

In the summer of 2000, British Airways once again took a bold leap into the future. Challenging the entire industry, the airline introduced a completely new concept for the business-class section of its long-haul fleet. The change in the cabin layout was amazing: the configuration is 2+2+2 across the wide-body, twin-aisle aircraft. The

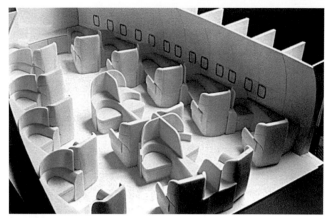

Courtesy British Airways

Courtesy British Airways

seats, or capsules, are positioned in pairs, each consisting of one seat facing forward and one facing the rear of the aircraft, and each seat converts into a 72-inch (1.83-metre), fully flat bed. At each position, there is an adjustable footstool, an adjustable headrest with movable neck support, a movable privacy screen, a personal power-supply outlet for laptop computers, and a video screen offering multi-channel entertainment. On-board stowage space for carry-on bags has been greatly increased, and the allowance per passenger has been raised to 39.68 pounds (18 kilograms).

As with the airline's first-class product, the new British Airways business-class beds are carefully designed to meet the requirements of North Atlantic business travellers.

To some passengers, the 'protective brace position' of the rear-facing seats seemed strange at first: they were asked to sit well back in their seats, with their hands crossed over the centre of their chests. Some critics predicted that commercial airline passengers would want to fly only feet first, as they have for many years. But, if we look at the history of military air transport, it is considered normal, and some say safer, for people to fly facing the rear of the aircraft. In the 1970s, on the Trident 2 aircraft, half the passengers flew backward and half did not – imagine the eye contact – and this configuration has a long tradition in other modes of transportation, for example on buses, boats and trains (see Chapter 15/Upgrades:Refurbishing Aloft, Alaska Airlines).

It took some time for the competition to catch up with the revolutionary Club World product launched by British Airways in 2000. However, two years later Singapore Airlines announced the introduction of its new Raffles Class SpaceBed, a US$100-million upgrade programme. Inaugurated on the Singapore–Hong Kong–Las Vegas route in the summer of 2002, this ultra-upmarket product is advertised as the industry's most spacious business-class sleeper seat, measuring 78 inches (1.98 metres) when fully extended.

Courtesy British Airways

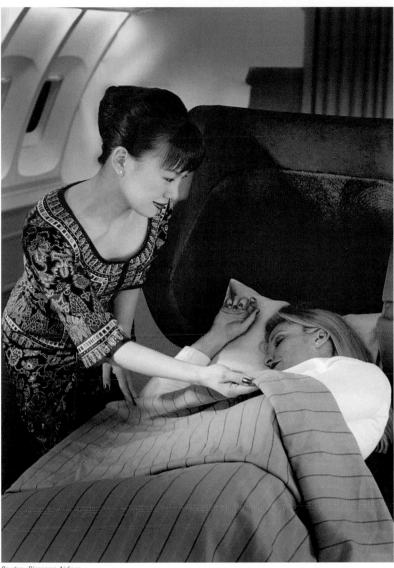

*How to relax on a long flight (information about the distinctive uniform worn by the flight attendant is provided in Chapter 13/Flying Colours)*

## SHORT-HAUL SERVICES

On short-haul routes, all too often there seems to be very little benefit to show for the relatively expensive business-class fare levels. Usually, the business-class cabin is configured to have fewer seat rows than economy class, so there is likely to be less noise and general disturbance. However, with the 'fixed movable dividers', which are positioned to divide the aircraft cabin in accordance with the specific number of passengers flying on a particular service on a particular day, it is possible for business travellers to find themselves part of a very large group. On certain flights, for example on the classic business routes, the number of economy-class passengers might indeed be far smaller than the number in business class.

Often, all the seats on the short-haul aircraft are the same size, with the same limited amount of leg room, which only serves to encourage complaints from business executives who represent the revenue core of the aviation industry and have paid extra for a greater level of comfort and more attention from the flight attendants than passengers who have paid a lower fare and who are sitting in the economy-class cabin.

It is true that airlines usually try to make up for lack of spaciousness on short-haul services by offering an enhanced food-and-beverage service, such as free drinks, two- or three-course meals with a choice of meal options and, sometimes, a hot main course. However, one of the main advances in improving comfort for business travellers has been the introduction of the '3-to-2/2-to-3' convertible seats that are widely used on European air services but, surprisingly, have not appeared as frequently on the US routes. This ingenious seating combination offers an airline the option of rapidly reconfiguring the aircraft to accommodate a varying product mix of business- and economy-class passengers. When the two-seat version is utilized, two business-class passengers will have the equivalent of one rather small empty seat between them – an ideal space for newspapers or laptop computers. In the economy-class cabin, the three-seat version of the convertible seating will accommodate three passengers sitting abreast, all in seats of equal size. In this way, product differentiation can be maintained, and business-class customers on the short-haul routes can be assured of superior levels of comfort.

In recent years, on short-haul aircraft there have also been moves to install power-supply outlets, TV screens and telephones – enhancements that previously tended to be associated with the larger aircraft flying on the long-haul routes.

## GLOBAL PERSPECTIVES

All these upgrades are helping to provide a more professional environment for business travellers worldwide. Indeed, there has been great progress since the early 1980s when Pan Am, a three-class carrier, pioneered Clipper Class, the first dedicated business-class cabin. The concept rapidly caught on. By the end of the decade, when SAS advertised its EuroClass cabin, the product features were already solidly in place; the airline's brochure stated, 'Work Class by day; Sleep Class by night . . . Most of all, you get peace and quiet. No movie. No smoking. No service (unless, of course, you insist)'. Sitting in normal seats, but with increased leg room, passengers were wrapped in duvets and 'sleeping collars' for the long night flights – a hitherto undreamed of level of comfort. But as they snoozed peacefully, were these aerial road warriors aware that they were, in fact, ushering in the dawn of a new age of business travel?

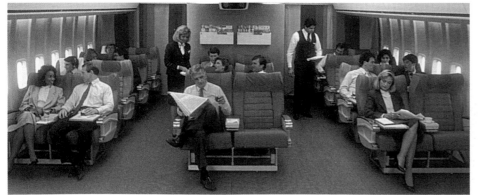

Courtesy Pan Am/George Design Studio

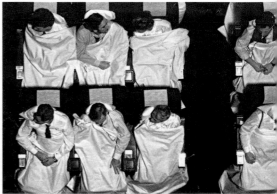

Courtesy SAS

Courtesy Continental

Courtesy United

## COMMENTS FROM THE SPECIALISTS

### Michael M Boland

*President and CEO, Maritz Travel Company, Chesterfield, Missouri*

The evolution of business-class service has created a product that is often better than the first-class product of only a few years ago – reclining seats, on-board entertainment and choice of meals. For the commercial market, the airlines' creation of the 'business/first' cabin met the travel policy guidelines of many corporations. It provides a very fine service that leaves the passengers feeling they're in first-class in an open environment with no one sitting in front of them.

In the world of incentive travel, where companies reward their top producers, truly special awards such as African photo safaris or tours of China often include the comfort of business-class travel, even for groups of more than a hundred award winners.

### Lamberto G Moris

*Design Principal, SMWM, San Francisco, California*

These comments describe our work for American Airlines at the time of the development of the business-class cabin for the Boeing B777.

It was emphasized that the new interiors must reflect the brand identity of American Airlines, particularly the shiny, clean image of its aircraft in the skies – the sleek, silver 'bird'. The designers, SMWM, were charged with developing the cabin interior pro-gramme in such a way as to incorporate elements of the exterior livery – the red, blue and platinum palette of colours and materials. Initially, SMWM identified the curvilinear shape of the plane as a unique interior space type, singular in its organic form. Nearly all buildings and human habitats are rectilinear, transportation modes being an exception. So the design team drew inspiration from other forms of transportation, including yachts, automobiles, railcars and early airplanes. The common threads established were the aero-dynamic, curvilinear forms and the implied luxury associated with historic rail, sea and air travel.

In order to meet the time schedule and technical requirements, SMWM pursued the work with two design teams – the overall cabin team and the seat team. The cabin-design team established the overall look of the plane interiors by starting with these curvi-linear forms, bringing the curve into the design of the bulkheads, decorative Tedlar laminates, carpeting, curtains and fabric uphol-steries, and the exterior livery of the airline into the cabin in the form of blue upholsteries, platinum trims on sidewalls and bulk-heads, and red accents for accessory items.

For business class, the seat was the paramount element. The seat-design team developed a seat with a fresh new look, slender and athletic, ergonomically responding to the form of the human body. The seat and back pans are upholstered in custom-designed wool fabric, and the headrest, side panels and seat trims are upholstered in deep blue leather.

### Barbara Bermack

*Travel Consultant, Mercury International Travel, New York*

Most carriers do not operate a domestic business-class service in the United States. First and coach, or 'business/first' and coach, are the norm. Some carriers have extended this formula to inter-national flights. These are the carriers of choice for my clients who are concerned about their comfort as well as the approval of their corporate finance departments. The product offered is very similar to first class but at business-class prices.

For the majority of travellers, business class is still too expen-sive, but for corporate travellers it is a perk of the status they have achieved in their companies. I have directives authorizing business class for flights of more than four hours, for instance. In this age of trying to be productive 24/7, it's perceived as the easiest way to arrive at a destination ready to work, without having to shake off the discomfort of jet lag and the exhaustion of coach travel.

Leisure travellers are now getting to experience business class in an unusual marketing agreement. Upscale cruise lines and tour operators are offering their clients business-class seats at greatly reduced fares that tie into their packages. International travel agencies specializing in high-end corporate travel have formed organizations, such as Virtuoso, that can negotiate special leisure packages appealing to their clientele.

Courtesy Qantas

Courtesy Qantas

Courtesy Qantas

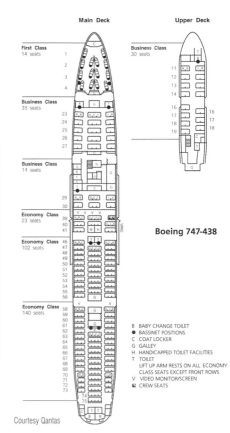

**Main Deck**

**Upper Deck**

**First Class**
14 seats

**Business Class**
30 seats

**Business Class**
35 seats

**Business Class**
14 seats

**Economy Class**
23 seats

**Economy Class**
102 seats

**Economy Class**
140 seats

**Boeing 747-438**

B  BABY CHANGE TOILET
●  BASSINET POSITIONS
C  COAT LOCKER
G  GALLEY
H  HANDICAPPED TOILET FACILITIES
T  TOILET
   LIFT UP ARM RESTS ON ALL ECONOMY
   CLASS SEATS EXCEPT FRONT ROWS
V  VIDEO MONITOR/SCREEN
☒  CREW SEATS

Courtesy Qantas

# Chapter 3
## ECONOMY-CLASS VALUE

*How much does it cost? On the New York–London route, at the turn of the millennium, the economy-class round trip published fare on both a three-class carrier and a two-class carrier was nearly US$1400. 'Bargain' fares were available at about half that amount. What can these passengers expect for their money? And how does it feel to fly in the economy-class salons in the sky?*

When customers buy economy-class tickets they expect to get the best possible *value* for their money. In the economy-class cabin they want to receive a warm, friendly welcome. In recent years they have started to look for evidence of product improvements that will distinguish their chosen carrier from the competition, for example, seat-back TV sets and telephones.

The 1980s and early 1990s saw dramatic product upgrades designed to appeal to first-class and business-class passengers. For the high-yield market segments, seat pitch was greatly increased, and entire seat rows were removed, enabling premium passengers to stretch out and relax. For economy-, tourist- or coach-class passengers, however, the cabin environment at this time remained relatively unchanged.

### CLOSE ENCOUNTERS

On short-haul aircraft, passengers who are squeezed into economy class know that after an hour or two they will be getting off the aircraft and will be able to stretch their legs and relax. However, for adults on long-haul aircraft, the economy-class experience can be unpleasant: the seat width between the armrests is often only 17 to 18 inches (43.18 to 45.72 centimetres); armrests are usually about 2 inches (5.08 centimetres) wide, unpadded and hard on the elbows; leg room, knee room and under-seat baggage stowage space is limited; and very few airlines provide footrests.

In addition, when there is a large movie screen flickering at the front of the cabin it is impossible to read in comfort; some airlines charge for entertainment headsets; there are not many food options; and some airlines charge US$4 to US$5 for alcoholic beverages.

In the early days of mass tourist travel, the surfaces of the seat backs and seat cushions tended to be very flat, with practically no lumbar support or contouring at the headrest area. It was distressing for passengers to find that those adjacent to them, while sleeping, had inadvertently fallen sideways – across their shoulders and knees! – and many passengers found it impossible to relax during long flights.

A number of consumer groups have accused the airlines of running a 'cattle-class' product. However, airlines counter this claim by pointing to the incredibly low promotional economy-class fares that are on offer. Though the bargain-basement approach was previously almost always linked to the traditional holiday-season dates, this situation has changed and newspapers now carry huge advertisements for 'Unique, Once-in-a-Lifetime, Low Fare Offers' virtually every day of the year. In some cases, passengers have reported that an Atlantic air fare can actually be cheaper than the combined price of the four taxi fares between the city centre and the airport at each end of the route.

### PERSONAL SPACE

Despite all the tariff hooplas, even now the normal economy-class seat-pitch measurements on many airlines are still 31 inches (78.74 centimetres) or 32 inches (81.28 centimetres) – unchanged from the last decades of the previous millennium. Some charter operators fly with economy-class seat rows at a pitch of 28 or 29 inches (71.12 or 73.66 centimetres), even on long-haul routes. For passengers regularly flying the North Atlantic route, this would be considered uncomfortable. But for routes where the passengers are generally of smaller stature – for example in the Far or Middle East – some airline managements have argued that a pitch of 29 or 30 inches (73.66 or 76.20 centimetres) is sufficient.

In recent years, specially contoured slimline seats, with flat, bungee-elastic web seat-back literature pockets and carved-out foams at knee level, have helped to provide greater comfort for economy-class passengers. Yet these extra features have created a blurring of the differentials between the various pitch measurements, as advertised by individual carriers, for the 'back of the bus'. When an airline proudly states that it flies 34-inch (86.36-centimetre) pitch in economy class, the passengers might find themselves sitting on heavily upholstered, old-style seats that offer less knee room than the new-style slimline seats that are positioned in a configuration with a pitch measurement of about 32 inches (81.28 centimetres).

## RECONCILING CLASS DIFFERENTIALS

At the turn of the millennium, however, there was a major change for the better. Some of the trends that had dominated cabin planning for first class and business class over the previous 20 years began to make their way into the economy-class cabin. Product features that at one time had been regarded as special 'goodies' offered exclusively to first-class passengers had, for reasons of competition, moved into business class where they became fixtures, or standard items. We are now seeing a similar process whereby a number of these significant product upgrades are being offered to passengers in the economy-class cabin.

At the individual economy-class seat positions, many leading international airlines now advertise the following features:

- larger overhead stowage bins with easy-access drop-down lids, providing increased space for passengers' carry-on baggage;
- winged headrests with movable neck support;
- improved seat contouring to provide greater lumbar support;
- better seat cushions constructed using foam layers of varying densities to counteract the problems of passenger slide-off and cushion compression;
- footrests, sometimes projecting forward from the passenger's seat at ankle level, sometimes projecting back from the seat in front of the passenger, or sometimes both;
- partitioned seat-back literature pockets;
- padded armrests;
- seat-back TV and video;
- power-supply outlets for computers;
- amenity kits;
- free headsets and entertainment;
- complimentary beverage service; and
- imaginative meal options that go beyond the old-style 'leather or feather' – that is, beef or chicken.

Courtesy Pan Am/George Design Studio

Courtesy British Airways

*Economy-class seating layouts from the 1980s*

*LEFT: In-flight entertainment, 1980s-style. Nowadays, economy-class passengers enjoy a far greater range of options including individually operated seat back TV sets (as shown at the beginning of this Chapter)*

Courtesy Pan Am/George Design Studio

Courtesy British Airways

*The distinctive styling of the aisle-side side panel of the British Airways World Traveller Plus seat helps ensure that this section of the aircraft will be immediately recognizable and clearly differentiated from the rest of the economy-class cabin (the market positioning of this product is explained in this Chapter)*

In addition, there is a distinct trend toward making the flying experience more closely resemble that of the higher-yield cabins where the passenger count is far smaller. In the old days, the wide-body, twin-aisle aircraft had large cabin areas for the large numbers of economy-class passengers. The flying experience was not unlike being in a cinema, theatre or lecture hall. But in recent times great emphasis has been placed on creating smaller, compartmentalized sections. Obviously, for revenue reasons, the basic seating configuration patterns – sometimes up to 10 abreast – have to be maintained. However, the overall cabin areas can be subdivided by installing partitions or 'monuments' (quasi-permanent fixed structural components such as coat closets, galleys, lavatories and bar counters), spaced at suitable intervals, or by using different colour schemes. Passengers tend to feel more comfortable when they are seated in smaller groups, rather than being 'lost', or 'submerged', in a huge crowd of people in a relatively large area.

## CLASS DISTINCTION

At long last, there are even signs of improvement in economy-class pitch measurements, largely due to changes in the buying habits of the business-travel market segment. No doubt leisure travellers might think that it is very pleasant to get extra leg room when they take off for their holidays, but the real reason for this improved level of comfort has nothing to do with vacation playgrounds. Instead it has everything to do with corporate travel budgets, and with the systematic cutbacks during the late 1990s. During those years, with fears of recession around the corner, many companies introduced new travel policies that dictated that for flights of, say, six hours or less, junior or mid-level executives must fly in economy class. The swing away from business class rapidly gathered momentum: in 2000, the International Air Transport Association (IATA) reported that approximately half of all business travellers were flying in economy class.

In some ways this parallels the change that occurred when corporate travel policies banned all but the very top executives from flying in the first-class cabin (see Chapter 2/Business-Class Comfort). Basically, first-class air fares were deemed too high for 'ordinary' mortals. So during the 1990s, in order to attract as many premium passengers as possible, the airlines competed to upgrade their business-class cabins. Now, in the new millennium, because business-class fares are considered prohibitively high, the airlines are once again competing ferociously against one another, only this time to upgrade their economy-class cabins, though this kind of upgraded accommodation is usually on offer only to passengers who have paid the full economy-class fare.

Courtesy United Express/Atlantic Coast Airlines

*This executive-style colour scheme can make the cabin of a 50-seat, all-economy-class Bombardier Regional Jet look like a corporate- or privately owned luxury business aircraft, or even like a Concorde (the evolution of this aesthetic approach is described in this Chapter; see also Chapter 14/Concorde Unique)*

## IMPROVEMENTS ALL ROUND

For example United, a 'traditional' three-class carrier offering first-class, business-class and economy-class service, has opened the first few rows of economy class – referred to as United Economy Plus and offering pitch increased by an extra 5 inches (12.70 centimetres) – to suitably qualified, frequently travelled repeat customers on a first-come, first-served basis. And Virgin Atlantic, which for a number of years was a 'new-style' two-class carrier flying Upper Class and economy class, introduced Premium Economy Class, effectively changing its status to three-class, but with a different traffic mix than that of carriers such as United.

The Virgin Atlantic sales brochure for Premium Economy Class emphasizes:

- the separate cabin;
- seats that are longer and wider than its regular economy-class seats – the pitch on the Boeing B747-400 is 38 inches (96.52 centimetres);
- increased knee room, leg room and headrest comfort;
- a pre-flight glass of champagne;
- a personal TV screen, with a minimum of six channels showing at least eight movies; Nintendo and PC games; the Sky Map aircraft tracker; the in-flight magazine *Hot Air*

and a selection of newspapers;

- a choice of three meals, including a vegetarian option; and
- fresh fruit available throughout the flight.

British Airways (a traditional three-class carrier) introduced World Traveller Plus, which creates, in effect, a fourth class of service, with all four classes travelling on board the same aircraft. This special seating area, for up to 40 passengers, is located between business class and economy class, and the configuration has a pitch of 38 inches (96.52 centimetres). The fare is 20 per cent higher than the normal economy-class fare. In addition to the extra seat width and leg room, at each position there are headrests and footrests, a power-supply outlet for laptops, and a telephone. These passengers have a double cabin baggage allowance. In 2001 British Airways reported that this product accounted for a third of all the airline's business.

But in the boldest move of all, American Airlines, the world's largest airline, removed rows of seats from all its economy-class cabins. Early in 2002 American reported that it had increased its economy-class pitch from 31 to 32 inches (78.74 to 81.28 centimetres) to an average of 34 to 35 inches (86.36 to 88.90 centimetres). It instantly became famous as the only airline to have expanded the available amount of leg room for all passengers across the entire economy-class (coach) section

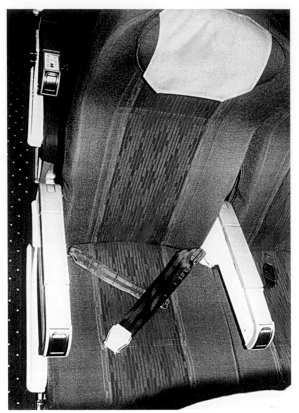

*During the 1990s, many airlines introduced monochromatic decor treatments in their economy-class cabins to replace the livelier, more vibrant colour combinations so very popular in earlier decades*

of its fleet. The project was named 'More Room', and branded 'More Room Throughout Coach'®. The implementation cost was more than US$70 million.

There was speculation among aviation specialists about whether other airlines would follow the example set by this enormous carrier. Economy-class passengers, naturally, were hopeful that airlines worldwide would make up for the years of discomfort they had inflicted on their 'steerage-class' market segment. Sadly, the other major airlines did not immediately choose to emulate American, so it remains to be seen whether, at some later stage, this dramatic – and most welcome – improvement will eventually be established as an industry norm.

Given the existence of these major product improvements, business travellers who have paid the full economy-class fare no longer want to sit alongside passengers who may have paid only a fraction of that amount. In particular, harried executives try to avoid those leisure passengers for whom the flight itself might be a kind of party experience. With this new mix of traffic, the task now facing the airlines is how best to manage the future of the economy-class cabin, and this is now the main industry battlefield.

## GOING UPMARKET

Not surprisingly, the style of cabin decor schemes for economy class has started to swing away from the traditional tourist-type, brightly coloured schemes that date from the 1970s and the early 1980s. There is a general shift toward using more serious, professional-looking colour combinations – strong, monochromatic treatments, particularly blues and greys. In 2000, when jetBlue launched its low-cost, low-fare, all-one-class, no-frills service, it advertised prominently that it was flying very sophisticated grey all-leather seat covers, from the nose to the tail of the aircraft, thereby creating a business-style ambience in the cabins of its Airbus A320 fleet.

In 1997, when United Express/Atlantic Coast Airlines prepared to take delivery of its first fleet of 50-seat Regional Jets from Bombardier, the decision was made to develop a dignified corporate-style design scheme that would befit its status as the largest operator on the East Coast of the United States, based at Dulles International Airport serving Washington, DC. Regional airlines are the fastest growing segment of commercial aviation and the new design scheme constituted a key element in the carrier's development strategy. The main planks of the design platform were that the decor be: clean and contemporary; professional,

Courtesy United

*An office-type ambience used to be the distinguishing feature associated specifically with business-class cabins. By the late 1990s, however, the executive 'look' (as described in this Chapter) had made its way into economy class. At the turn of the millennium, industry reports showed that more than half of all business-travel miles flown were in the economy-class cabin, and it is possible that this trend could continue in the foreseeable future (other related air transport statistics are provided in Chapter 16/Ways Ahead)*

businesslike, subtle, refined and stylish. The requirement was for the overall look to be akin to that of the Concorde interiors; after all, the cross-section dimensions of the Regional Jet 50-seat cabin do not differ greatly from those of one Concorde cabin. (At the time, both the Air France and British Airways Concorde fleets were flying grey decor schemes).

United Express/Atlantic Coast Airlines selected mid-grey and dark blue as the main colours for its new interior decor scheme – very different from the bright red-and-pink striped patterns flying on their Jetstream fleets at the time. Though the airline had hoped to fly leather seat covers, an edict from the very highest level of the company prevented the use of leather in the aircraft interior. The solution was to use a special aviation-grade fabric: the colour was mid-grey, and it had a grained, rippled surface, picked out with a scattering of tiny, near-invisible yellow dots. With lines of horizontal 'channelling' stitched firmly across the central area of the seat back, this fabric succeeded in looking as serious and as solid as leather, particularly when the neon lights throughout the cabin were switched on at full strength. The seat itself was upholstered in the 'cathedral style', in that a few extra inches of height were added at the headrest area in order to make the seat resemble an executive's chair in a corporate office. The

use of dark blue for the curtains and the vertical surfaces of the cabin dividers, plus a carpet streaked in a combination of dark-grey shades, made the overall presentation resemble that of a high-class business jet.

For an all-economy-class regional short-haul feeder carrier, this was a major statement of its intention to develop, and run, a superior product. On 23 March 1998 *Commuter/Regional Airline News* reported that United Express/Atlantic Coast Airlines had 'carved out [its] identity at Dulles, but not at the expense of partner United'. There were, in fact, two operations: the feeder services for the mega-carrier and the airline's own regional services. The new look needed to cover both missions, but there was no time in between flights to effect a change in the decor scheme, for example different seat-cover fabrics. The challenge, then, was how to switch identity from one airline to the other in the time available. The answer lay in swapping headrest covers. When flying as United Express, the carrier displayed the United 'tulip' insignia on headrest covers that were made of the same fabric as the seat covers; when flying as Atlantic Coast Airlines, the carrier used contrasting dark blue headrest covers displaying the initials ACA. This type of change-out can be handled easily during an overnight stay in the hangar, or by flight attendants during a

Courtesy Singapore Airlines

Courtesy United

Courtesy SAS

turnaround while the aircraft is parked at the airport departure gate.

Across the industry, there are now clear signs of a new sense of mission for the economy-class product: it must now offer better value than ever before. Consequently, all economy-class passengers stand to benefit. It is time for new thinking, and a new look. It is unlikely that, in the next decade or so, we shall see a return to those spots, squiggles and wild floral patterns that used to run riot across economy-class bulkheads. And all because of those frugal, hardworking business executives – and the cutbacks in their corporate travel budgets!

## COMMENTS FROM THE SPECIALISTS

### Lamberto G Moris
*Design Principal, SMWM, San Francisco, California*
These comments describe our work for American Airlines at the time of the development of the main (economy-class) cabin for the Boeing B777.

The airline and its design team, SMWM, wanted to ensure visual continuity from one service level to the next, while reflecting the differences in cost/value and the greater extent of space within the main cabin. The overall cabin-design team brought the major surface elements from first and business class into the main cabin via carpeting, sidewall treatments, bulkheads and curtains. The main differences are in the seats, which are upholstered in a brighter blue fabric that works better in the larger, lighter space of the main cabin. To advance the notion of more luxury in coach class, the six-way adjustable headrests are upholstered in blue leather.

As in business class, the main cabin seat was the most prominent element. The seat-design team worked to create a sleekly curved seat, one with less bulk, for a more streamlined style and to maximize the width and leg space. Amenities include power-supply outlets and individual video screens.

### Barbara Bermack
*Travel Consultant, Mercury International Travel, New York*
Most travellers, by necessity, travel in coach (economy) class. The cost difference between coach and business and/or first class, both domestically and internationally, is so great that it has become virtually unattainable for most travellers to experience the front of the plane.

It is in coach that airlines really differentiate themselves. One of the most successful of the new airlines, jetBlue, started flying all-coach planes with relatively comfortable seats and personal entertainment units, albeit with no food service. But the flight attendants are extremely courteous and the ground crews helpful. Clients coming off these planes were eager to fly jetBlue again.

In order to compete, the established airlines began providing more leg room in their coach sections, and offering personal entertainment centres, footrests and more comfortable seat cushions. It's really all being driven by market share, and jetBlue has made inroads on routes that were once dominated by the big airlines.

On international routes, carriers such as Virgin Atlantic and British Airways began upgrading their coach sections long before other carriers saw the need for this service. Both instituted a 'preferred coach' section, which offered a larger seat and more leg room, as well as enhanced food service. What's more, they have priced these products – called Premium Economy or World Traveller Plus – well; for only a few hundred dollars more these sections have become a haven for corporate travellers who are prohibited from flying in any section but coach. US carriers have scrambled to add these enhancements as well, just to keep up with the competition.

### Michael M Boland
*President and CEO, Maritz Travel Company, Chesterfield, Missouri*
One of the most successful and consistent economy-class services implemented by an airline, in my view, has been accomplished by Southwest Airlines. First, Southwest offers a less complex product to fewer market segments or customers. Second, it has been a master at managing customer expectations – you get what you pay for. On a three-hour flight on Southwest you are thrilled when they offer you a shrink-wrapped beef stick, but disappointed with a cold sandwich on a one-hour flight from a mega-carrier.

Southwest has also done a tremendous job of developing and keeping a consistent look; its aircraft, all Boeing B737s, have the same interior and exterior livery. The staff uniforms – in-flight and on the ground – have a consistent style: shorts, polo shirts, bomber jackets, etc. And, most important, Southwest's people – the face of the brand – reflect the style of the airline, as embodied by long-time Chairman Herb Kelleher – friendly, humble and efficient.

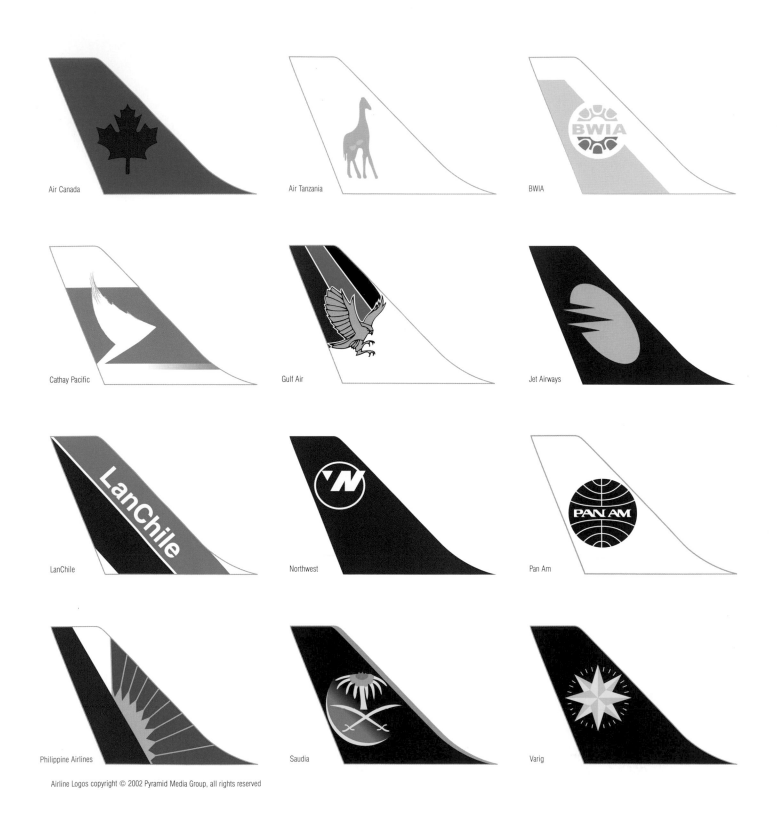

Air Canada

Air Tanzania

BWIA

Cathay Pacific

Gulf Air

Jet Airways

LanChile

Northwest

Pan Am

Philippine Airlines

Saudia

Varig

*In the hangar paint bays, detailed design patterns on the tail fins of aircraft were traditionally painted by hand – a painstaking and often lengthy process that could involve a complicated series of masks and stencils. During the 1980s, however, airlines started to make greater use of stick-on 'decals' (for example, the British Airways coat of arms shown later in this Chapter). This approach can speed up the process and reduce overall aircraft 'downtime', consequently achieving significant cost savings on a year-round basis*

# Chapter 4
## AERO IDENTITY

*What are the benefits airlines derive from their identity schemes and corporate branding programmes? Why are they important? How can added value be communicated within the passenger cabin?*

With the advent of the major alliances during the 1990s (oneworld, Qualiflyer, SkyTeam and Star), the individual participating airlines stated publicly that they would work toward harmonization of standards and resources – 'seamless service'. For example, cost savings can be achieved through a joint supply chain in the big-budget areas such as manufacturers' parts, the purchase of jet fuel and catering. But for passengers it remained to be seen whether there would be attempts to develop common branding or corporate-image programmes for jetliner cabins worldwide.

So far, this has not been the case, and the concept of an all-encompassing display of global decor schemes for a group of cooperating airlines is likely to remain a distant dream for the time being. Indeed, in the past few years, in all parts of the world, we have seen airlines taking steps to upgrade and clarify their *individual* company images. Once considered the preserve of the specialists in the advertising and design departments, a good corporate branding programme (CBP) is now accepted as an essential part of an airline's overall corporate marketing strategy.

### CORPORATE BRANDING PROGRAMMES

Customers tend to associate corporate branding programmes purely with the cosmetic aspects of the visual presentation of a product range. However, at a strategic level branding is a way of managing change in the marketplace. An effective CBP will:

- communicate the character, goals, values and market positioning of the parent organization;
- represent consistent standards of quality and employee behaviour – a prerequisite for developing and retaining customer loyalty; and
- clearly state what the organization is, what it does and what it is planning to become (classic, modern, futuristic, snappy, dynamic, world-beater, cut-throat, lovable, reliable, etc).

In aviation, a CBP is generally expressed in the unique combination of colours, names, logos and symbols the organization has chosen to use to distinguish itself from competing brands. There is a clear need for airlines to run an efficient CBP in order to meet all regulatory requirements and to ensure a practical level of design consistency, commonality and uniformity across the key visual aspects of the business, for example aircraft interiors and exteriors, flight-service equipment, employee uniforms, ground vehicles, properties and facilities, ticket offices, airport check-in desks, arrival and departure areas, VIP lounges, graphics, signage, documentation, stationery and printed material.

Without a CBP, an organization is in danger of becoming a 'nonentity' – an undifferentiated commodity. It will almost certainly suffer from fragmentation and inconsistency, and the resulting variation in standards will cause confusion and distress among

Courtesy Star Alliance

Courtesy Star Alliance

51

FIRST CLASS

BUSINESS CLASS

ECONOMY CLASS

Menu

Courtesy South African Airways

*This corporate branding programme encompassed all three classes of service simultaneously (details are provided in this Chapter)*

Courtesy Lufthansa

Courtesy Lufthansa

*The subtle diagonal stripes woven into the grey seat-cover fabric recall the graceful flight angle of the crane that appears on the tail fins of Lufthansa aircraft*

customers and employees alike. Business opportunities will be lost. Brand value will be destroyed. It will become increasingly difficult to realize cost savings from economy of scale or presentation of critical mass. Money, time and effort will be wasted. Ultimately, the organization will find itself at a competitive disadvantage, forced to compete via a potentially fatal downward spiral of price-cutting.

## SETTING UP THE CBP

*Stage 1 – Top Management*. When it is time for an organization to upgrade an existing CBP or establish a new CBP, the impetus has to come from top management. The vision, mission and objectives of the organization need to be agreed upon and stated, then promoted and 'sold' to the work force. Without a wholehearted commitment from all quarters, it is unlikely that there will be a great deal of progress. For any airline embarking on a CBP, it is essential to take into account from the very outset the mandated regulatory requirements that will govern all stages of the decision-making process (see Chapter 15/Upgrades: Refurbishing Aloft).

*Stage 2 – Advertising and Design Agencies*. Working from the platform communicated by top management, these agencies define the scope and the basic elements of the corporate marks and signature and establish the colour policies for the overall programme. Assessing input and feedback from throughout the organization (for example, from marketing, engineering, maintenance, logistics and operations), they define a corporate scheme that will

be certifiable (that is, one that will meet all regulatory requirements in the areas of safety, security, flammability, burn rate, heat release, smoke, toxicity, etc) and maintainable within the normal practical working capabilities of the organization.

*Stage 3 – In-House Departments*. Taking on responsibility to ensure compliance with all mandated regulatory requirements, the controllers and the general managers develop the CBP implementation plan. They move to:

- organize the budget, time frame, and action plans for background and display applications;
- establish the core material for use by the specialist work teams throughout the organization;
- initiate the process of communication with the work force, the trade and the public;
- develop and run the supporting programmes;
- issue launch statements, to be passed on to:
    regulatory authorities;
    central, regional, and local government;
    customers, both direct and indirect;
    investment analysts, bankers and stockbrokers;
    shareholders, pensioners and trade unions;
    local media companies;
    journalists and influential opinion leaders;
    associated trade and industry organizations;
    training and educational establishments, etc.

*Airline corporate branding programmes feature a dazzling range of pictorial design elements. Among the most popular selections are: emblems and colour combinations associated with the country where the airline is based; examples of local flora and fauna; memorable motifs and insignia; directional and geometric patterns; acronyms and beloved icons (the logos in this Chapter are shown with the kind permission of the named airlines)*

*Launched in December 1984 at the time when the airline was preparing for privatization, the British Airways corporate identity programme was the largest of its kind in aviation history (the key design elements are described in this Chapter)*

Courtesy British Airways

### The CBP and the aircraft interior

Given that airline passengers spend their money to sit *inside* an aircraft, it is astonishing that so much attention tends to be given to the programmes for fleet *exteriors*. It is a requirement that each airline's paint scheme be unique. However, this topic also generates very powerful emotions: presidents, prime ministers, royalty, politicians, chiefs of industry, film stars and assorted 'experts' all seem to have plenty to say about what should or should not be featured in the livery paint scheme of the local airline. Individuality is treasured and chosen icons are displayed proudly in all parts of the world. It is ironic, however, that passengers who board aircraft via jetway bridges (the covered corridors – or 'fingers' – that extend from the airport terminal building to the door of the aircraft, as shown in Chapter 16/Ways Ahead) are unlikely to see anything more of the airline's aircraft exterior paint scheme than the few inches that surround the door aperture!

But when it comes to fleet *interior* schemes, these 'experts' have far less to offer. Bringing elements such as individual flag markings, or national flora or fauna, to the cabin interior presents a unique challenge that is easier to ignore and, no doubt, this is one of the main reasons that so many aircraft cabins seem to look the same. Some airlines display several colours of the rainbow on the tail fins of their aircraft but choose to use less dramatic colour schemes for their fleet interior programmes, opting

instead for something more 'safe' and restful. This in turn means that airlines need to find other ways to advertise their brand identity within the cabin, such as via meal-tray presentation, amenity kits, decorative wall treatments and so on.

For example, at South African Airways six dramatic colours are presented on the tail fins of the aircraft – each carrying a symbolic value and related to the graphic display on the national flag. During the planning of the airline's Millennium Interior programme, it was decided that two of the colours were to be selected as the main focus of the aircraft interior-design scheme – blue to represent the sky and the two oceans that cradle the country, and green to represent the land.

The aircraft interior was further enhanced by incorporating unique African motifs: in first class, the outline of a prized cycad plant on the rear-facing front cabin divider, with decorative walnut effects on the front-facing rear cabin divider and on the shell surrounds of the lie-flat sleeper seats; in business class, a sturdy baobab tree; and in economy class a friendly daisy. And for the purpose of continuity, a sequence of multi-ethnic, traditional tribal patterns was arranged in different formats to decorate items such as menu covers.

The overall effect, authentically and unmistakably representative of the Republic of South Africa, is not likely to be appropriated for use by any other carrier.

Courtesy British Airways

*This branding programme encompassed the entire organization including: city ticket offices; airport check-in desks, VIP lounges and boarding-gate areas; signage, graphics, corporate stationery and advertising copy; uniforms for all customer contact employees and ground workers; airport vehicles; and the exteriors and the interiors of all the aircraft in the fleet. Even relatively small items such as name-badges, bag-tags and headrest covers (shown above) were included in the action plan*

### Running a CBP

When an airline does manage to achieve a distinctive and fully coordinated brand image across the entire organization, the pay-off can be tremendous. During the mid-1980s, British Airways needed to prepare for privatization, a process that was uncharted territory for both the airline and the nation. To herald the transformation, the airline created a new look that was structured to appeal to both its customer base and to its future investors. The main objectives of the working brief issued to the advertising and design agencies included:

- the creation of a distinctive corporate identity that would make the airline stand out in the world marketplace;
- reflecting the new customer-service orientation in terms of colour and warmth;
- communicating a sense of professionalism and precision based on the strength of the airline's technical expertise; and
- demonstrating pride of origin as the British national flag-carrier.

In its day, this design programme was considered the most comprehensive – and expensive – in the history of aviation. The British Airways corporate signature consisted of three key visual elements: the Speedwing, or 'dramatic red flash', a thin red horizontal line that terminated in a broad diagonal stroke which appeared on aircraft exteriors and ground-handling equipment and was also used to designate aircraft interiors, properties, premises and facilities such as check-in desks and executive lounges, and for advertising messages, signage, stationery, documentation, name badges and so on; the logotype (the company name written in a specially designed typeface); and the coat of arms (inspired in part by the Union Jack and bearing the motto 'to fly to serve'). All aspects of the corporate visual image were closely coordinated to feature four specially graded colours: Speedwing red (a glowing cherry shade), midnight blue, pearl grey and silver. This colour palette was derived from the national flag, but the aim was to offer a look that was both richer and warmer than the bold, poster-style combinations that had dominated some of the earlier livery schemes. Within two years the programme had become uniquely successful from the standpoint of brand recognition, and subsequently rose to prominence as the prime industry benchmark.

### WHY NOW?

Branding is all about bonding with the customers – it is the heart and soul of the business – and a good brand image can make a difference to the survival of a company during difficult periods. Airlines such as Southwest and Virgin Atlantic are famous for having built up strong loyalty in the marketplace. Each offers its own specific range of product features and customer benefits. Their brand values are renowned, and they have worked hard to communicate their brand identities in order to attract their particular target groups of customers. Those customers who are attracted to the market positioning of these airlines and who come forward to buy their range of products are, in a way, pre-equipped with certain product expectations that these airlines are then able to satisfy. The end result is happy customers and return business.

However, at the beginning of the new millennium there are several trends in the airline industry that are threatening to annihilate individual identity. This is particularly true for distribution, where buyers are seeking only the most attractive *bargains* on the Internet and are not especially concerned about which airline they fly with. For individual airlines, therefore, there is now a greater need than ever before to clearly differentiate their specific brand positioning and style – and to communicate their *own* way of doing business.

### COMMENTS FROM THE SPECIALISTS

#### Philip George
*George Design Studio, Pine Plains, New York*

In my design experience with Braniff, Air Florida, Pan Am, Saudia and BWIA, I have found that the marketing and corporate-identity programmes are driven by competition. The corporate desire to improve and differentiate the product since deregulation has been forced by the severe route competition.

The birth of colour, drama and flair in air travel came about through the imagination of Mary Wells and her advertising team at the Jack Tinker Agency. The concept was initially presented to Continental, which had introduced multi-class cabins and had a reputation for innovative marketing. When Continental decided not to move ahead with the concept, Harding Lawrence, new at

Braniff, seized the opportunity to make a small regional carrier into a major force on the north–south routes.

The programme provided an entire generation of air travellers with the excitement of an air voyage using an approach that included virtually every element of the travel experience: colours, handsome fabrics, decorated side panels, leather seats, coordinated passenger amenities, chef-prepared menus, special amenities, installation of art and folk art in airports and ticket offices – the list was endless. It affected every way in which a passenger was in contact with Braniff during a trip.

In developing this programme and its successors for more than 20 years, I found that our familiarity with all levels of personnel, management, engineering and manufacturers helped my team to respond with unique and new innovations. For example, the introduction of leather in first class and subsequently in economy class had the benefit of providing the passenger with a luxury feel and the smell of a Mercedes, and allowed the airlines to lower their maintenance needs and eliminate the headrest covers. Every item the passenger touched or used in-flight was reviewed for improvement, subject to Federal Aviation Administration (FAA) approval and to Boeing or Airbus engineering constraints.

Prior to these innovations, it was the aircraft manufacturer who designed cabin interiors and it was the airline purchasers who had to press for new and innovative solutions to satisfy their own customers. Today, most major carriers have in-house design professionals or outside consultants to develop coordinated corporate-identity programmes that include all aircraft livery. Many carriers today have developed wild and crazy aircraft exterior markings to establish market identity, ideas that probably came from their advertising-agency art departments.

What has brought about the greying down of most aircraft interior livery? It seems to be playing to the lowest common denominator of passenger perceptions. Where, pray tell, is the idea that colour enlivens our environment, and lifts our spirits for the journey? Not all passengers are going to business meetings.

**Peter Sheahan**

*Sheahan & Associates, Scarsdale, New York*

Airlines – like many stressed individuals – have gone through an enduring identity crisis over the past several decades. At one time an international carrier traded heavily on its national-flag relationships, the attraction of its culture, and the proud loyalty of a home market. Indeed, route structures were so restricted that it made sense to actually promote destinations in and of themselves. What airline today produces free annual calendars, destination travel posters or guidebooks from its own budget?

With domestic deregulation in the United States and slower but equally relentless liberalization of international routes, market entry carriers have lost their unique destination identities. For a time, they could fall back on differentiating themselves with who had the first Boeing B747 or DC10 or who had the largest fleet of the newest and fastest aircraft on which nonstop routes. The focus on fleet development was on capacity and perceived performance differences. Again, this changed when commercial aircraft development ceased introducing revolutionary new wide-bodies with speed and range improvements, and began to focus more on incremental, evolutionary enhancements such as fuel economy and maintenance reliability – issues that are important but not of great interest to the travelling public.

Beyond the enormous impact of frequent-flyer programmes and price enticements, the airlines now seek to differentiate themselves by addressing individual passenger comfort. The trend is to promote seat pitch in economy class and expansive individualized comfort in business and first class. Think of the contrast today between the cocoon-like, almost womb-like first-class seats and the gregarious upstairs dining experience on Pan Am or the prevalence of bars on transcontinental flights in earlier decades. It seems that today only Virgin Atlantic makes a feature of promoting an environment of ambience among its passengers.

With most travel options restricted to similar aircraft at similar pricing and a wide selection of carriers, airlines will have to find the particular value that applies to the customer base they want to attract. These conditions of commonality in pricing, aircraft and scheduling are creating a commodity-like product, and are leading to a world in which a carrier may not be able to be all things to all customers.

# Passenger Experience

# Chapter 5
## SKY LIGHTS

*Cabin lighting systems have recently become very sophisticated, giving airline passengers more freedom to exercise control over their immediate surroundings. What has been the impact of this democratization process on the overall passenger experience?*

High above the steppes of Central Asia in the mid-1990s, on board a very elderly Russian-built aircraft, a flight attendant demonstrated the cabin lighting system: 'There's just this one switch. This is the totalitarian approach. It's easy: either all the lights are on or they're all off!' Although there were individual air-vent nozzles positioned on each seat back, there were no individual reading lights at all. The passengers seemed unperturbed; while many were snoozing, others were using their own personal flashlights to read or to make their way around the cabin.

At one time, many aircraft flew with just a small number of common, household-style, incandescent light bulbs – and very few switches. Subsequently came a move to fluorescent lamps, which were less heavy and provided greatly improved performance. Nowadays, airlines can draw on a wide range of high-tech options, including halogen, electroluminescence, fibre optics and light-emitting diodes (LEDs).

In the late 1990s, when United Express/Atlantic Coast Airlines was preparing for the first deliveries of its new fleet of Bombardier regional jets, it came as a surprise that the powerful neon lighting washed out a number of the traditional colour options that were under consideration for the cabin decor scheme. This was one of the reasons for the airline's decision to fly headrest covers in a rich shade of dark blue.

Concurrent with recent technological developments has been a marked change in the way in which cabin lighting systems are put to use. The transition from a central command control to the more democratic process passengers enjoy today did not occur overnight, nor was it achieved without a certain measure of trial and tribulation for the on-board populace.

Individual reading lights on narrow-body aircraft are still usually activated using overhead push-button switches located in the passenger service unit (PSU). However, accessibility to these switches is a problem for passengers with disabilities that impair movement, for anyone whose arm length does not conform exactly to the specified distance between the seat and the overhead panels, and for everyone when the tray-tables are deployed, laden with food, documents or laptop computers.

The introduction of touch-pad controls – horizontally, on the top

Courtesy Virgin Atlantic

Courtesy Continental

surface of the armrests – was initially viewed as a major break-through in cabin lighting design. Still, passengers lamented that an important area of their immediate personal storage space had been taken away from them, and when they banged down a book, an elbow or a cocktail glass they could – by mistake – activate their own or, embarrassingly, their fellow passengers' light switch, or even the flight-attendant call button. Furthermore, it did not help when chewing gum and beverages seeped into the crevices between the various buttons.

Later, these passenger control pads were installed vertically, on the inner surfaces of the armrests or on the seat side panels. Passengers regard this advance as a definite improvement until they have to request help with the control pad from a flight attendant – for example to adjust the recline mechanism – when some of them then complain that their thighs are being 'groped'.

## SHINE THE LIGHT

There has been a steady move to install individual gooseneck reading lights in first- and business-class cabins. This was a feature pioneered by British Airways in late 1995 when, to great acclaim, the airline launched its then revolutionary lie-flat first-class sleeper-seat pod compartments. During the early 1990s, many passengers had started to bring on board their own small reading lights in order to see clearly when they studied their computer printouts or when they used their 'luggable', and later their laptop, computers. The provision of an adjustable gooseneck light at each seat position represented a most welcome upgrade and demonstrated that the airline was paying close attention to developing trends and giving passengers a greater level of individual control over the lighting in their personal space.

This trend spread quickly from first to business class. On some carriers, for example Delta in its Business Elite cabin, United in its Business Class cabin and Virgin Atlantic in Upper Class, the necks, or stems, of these installations project from the framework of the seat.

At the end of the 1990s, in the wide-body, first-class cabins of long-haul carriers such as South African Airways, Swissair and United, gooseneck reading lights began to be installed in the 'furniture' adjacent to the seat, projecting from the console or the sideboard. Some experts contend that this is a more stable

Courtesy British Airways

location – less likely to result in entanglement with the wires of passenger earphones or headsets – and most airlines now use slide- or rocker-type switches for these installations (the mechanics of earlier controls were not so user-friendly). For easy switching of the individual overhead lights, the most popular solution so far seems to be the removable, handheld passenger control pad attached to the end of a retractable wire; passengers can lift this out from the 'insert' position on the inner side of the armrest panel and place it wherever they choose. The light switches are integrated with the controls of the in-flight entertainment system.

## MOOD SWING

While individual reading lights have helped give passengers greater personal control over their immediate environment, this represents only a *practical* improvement in the upgrade process. For overall *aesthetic* and *perceptual* improvements we have to look at the very recent developments in the field of 'mood lighting'.

According to Steve Jaffe, Vice President and General Manager of Bruce Industries, which designs and manufactures interior and exterior lighting for commercial aircraft, 'There is a growing trend in our industry to look beyond the usual engineering considerations and constraints that govern lighting system designs, with an eye to creating environments that enhance the passenger's experience.' For example, instead of having the old, factory-type lighting running in a snake-like sequence from the nose to the tail of the aircraft, it is now possible to offer a wide range of lighting treatments.

New lighting installations can be customized to produce special effects across the various sections of the aircraft, the way they are in hotels, retail outlets and leisure centres. For example:

- at entryways the lighting installation should provide a bright and welcoming ambience; careful use of sunny colours can help to create the impression of spaciousness;
- in lavatories, the lighting should provide a flattering glow for weary travellers;
- aircraft seats should have individual control pads to activate different lighting combinations; passengers need to be able to relax, eat, sleep, work and enjoy the in-flight entertainment systems without squinting or getting sore eyes;

*These photographs show examples of 'mood lighting' on board wide-body aircraft (the techniques and associated aesthetic benefits of which are described in this Chapter)*

- the closets and the overhead stowage bins should not resemble dingy locker rooms;
- galleys should look clean and hygienic;
- handrails in the cabin should be illuminated, as on the Boeing B717 aircraft.

To produce memorable effects, key product features can be highlighted in imaginative ways – at the work stations in the business centre, the counter of the duty-free shop, the manicure table in the beauty salon and the cocktail display in the bar corner.

**Mood-lighting programmes**

Virgin Atlantic has pioneered an exciting new approach by turning to theatrical-lighting experts for inspiration and guidance: the Upper Class (executive-style) cabin features a state-of-the-art lighting system that changes mood throughout the flight. Public Relations Manager Wendy Buck explains:

Our new lighting system is part of our US$100-million

Courtesy Virgin Atlantic

package of product and service improvements. It comple-ments the style of our aircraft livery paint scheme, which features shades of metallic silver, purple and red. Inside the cabin, our lighting programmes spotlight eight different moods, reflecting the different stages of the flight experi-ence – from dawn to dusk and from restaurant to lounge. Interior lighting has always played a key role in restaurants, bars and hotel reception areas, yet previously no airline had taken it seriously as part of the flying experience. By design-ing a changing lighting programme, we provide for our pas-sengers a realistic sense of the passage of time in a variable environment, which is activity appropriate and which ban-ishes the boredom of monolithic lighting schemes. Our approach to lighting is coordinated with the selection of colours and fabrics within the cabin to provide a completely integrated feel with each lighting option. The entire pro-gramme is themed around the 'Modern Romance of Flight'.

This gives our cabin a striking new look which reflects the romantic era of flying in the 1930s.

This new technology offers endless options – auras of luminosity in passionate purple and bubble-gum pink, can now be a normal part of the everyday flight experience. Instead of the traditional on/off lighting format, imagine slowly waking up or going to sleep to a 15-minute-long desert or mountain sunrise or sunset. Also available are new lighting installations that, instead of being bound by the traditional 30 per cent cutoff level, can fade smoothly down to less than 1 per cent of the total strength of the lights. And gel-wrapped bulbs nowadays provide a choice of more than 150 solid colours.

The special lighting settings for passenger boarding, meal times, sleeping, waking, disembarkation and so on can be controlled – that is, started and stopped – by the flight attendants on board the aircraft, and while the aircraft is on the ground the programmable system can be updated in minutes via personal computer.

## SAFETY MATTERS

With careful handling, there is no reason why these non-emergency lighting treatments should in any way compromise the safety-lighting and emergency escape-path lighting installations that are positioned throughout the aircraft. It can even be argued that, through the use of restful shades of pink, purple and blue for the general in-flight experience, passengers will be far more aware of the impact of the all-important warning signs that are displayed using the mandatory colours of red, green and yellow.

## THE FINAL FRONTIER

So how can airlines manage variations in the level of natural light admitted into the aircraft, for example due to the time of day, weather conditions and aircraft orientation? The long-haul fleet of South African Airways flies with window shades closed for well over 90 per cent of its flying hours; some of the time it is dark outside, and at other times the outside light is too bright because of the rising or setting sun. In the future it is likely that passengers will have yet another individual control point, to replace the single-panel push-up/pull-down window shades that have been in use for some 40 years. The cabin window shades of tomorrow might

well be electric-powered. At the touch of a button, passengers will be able to choose how much outside light they would like to let in – all, or none, or various amounts in between. And this system will permit airlines to customize their aircraft interiors in ways that were previously not possible.

## COMMENTS FROM THE SPECIALISTS

### Stan Sim

*Programme Manager, Aerosud Interiors (Pty) Ltd, Pierre van Ryneveld, Republic of South Africa*

Cabin lighting has changed the way airline-interior product developers, together with the cabin-interior engineers, study the cabin interior when making changes. The use of different lighting hues creates different cabin interior colouring, providing passengers with a new outlook on cabin interiors and making the flight experience a positive and lasting one.

In an example of different modes of lighting in the first-class cabin of a Boeing B747-400, a blue LED light was installed in the front of each ottoman (the 'footstool' located forward of the seat),

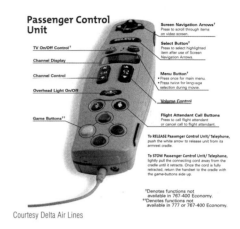

Courtesy Delta Air Lines

with the light shining down onto the carpet. The initial idea for this requirement was to create an ambience of peace and tranquillity for the passengers in the first-class cabin. The second was to provide subdued lighting, to assist the passenger when moving about in the cabin in the dark, when other lights were turned out. Both of these criteria were achieved with good success. The brightness of the light was toned down a little to reduce the amount of reflection in the cabin. However, this was not the only benefit of this type of lighting.

During the design phase of the cabin interior, the same light was used as an illumination device, to help prevent a front-row trip hazard on the centre seats. After the installation, there was an added advantage: the seats installed in the cabin gave the impression of floating above the floor. This was an optical effect created by the light, and it was a very striking in the cabin area. With a small investment and a real concern for the existing cabin environment, an exceptional ambience was created for the passengers and the cabin crew.

**Robert S Brown**
*Chief Executive Officer, SYAIR Designs LLC, Little Rock, Arkansas*

The attention and investment inside the cabin of the aircraft has principally been on seat improvements and product enhancements of in-flight entertainment systems – for example thin-screen LCDs, the introduction of DVDs and audio/video-on-demand. Little has changed in cabin lighting since the introduction of the fluorescent tube – until now. With the advancements in LED and fibre-optic technology, new products are being introduced in both the commercial- and private-aviation markets on all models of aircraft. The improvements in cabin lighting include the availability of a full colour spectrum of light, the ability to set any temperature of white light, significant weight and space savings and improved warranty and maintenance of the product.

There is not an aircraft manufacturer, major modification centre or airline that is not evaluating new cabin-lighting products. The result will be a needed improvement in client and customer satisfaction. The new lighting products and technologies now being developed and installed will offer cabin mood lighting, lavatory vanity lights, high bright reading lamps and new safety lighting. Within the cabin of the aircraft, lighting offers the greatest environmental improvement for a comfortable and relaxing flight.

# Chapter 6
## DINING À LA JET SET

*Do they drop down, pop up or slide forward? Passengers reach for their tray-tables the minute they see dining trolleys in the aisles. Transport catering can range from picnics to five-star service. How will jetliner diners fare in the new millennium?*

### TABLE D'HÔTE

In order to achieve urgently needed cost savings in the post-11 September 2001 operating environment, the major US carriers – with the exception of Continental – took a draconian stance, announcing huge cuts in meal services on domestic flights effective from 1 November 2001. In the first-class cabin they stopped serving meals on flights of under two hours. In economy class they stopped offering meal service on flights of under three and three-quarter hours. As the cost of food in economy class averages US$4 per head, this resulted in an immediate payoff for the airlines.

From the customers' point of view, however, this was a miserable moment in the history of aviation. The scary stories of flying coast to coast via two or three hubs with only peanuts, pretzels and a beverage for sustenance used to be standard fare in the repertoire of stand-up comedians. Now they are a reality.

Some passengers have retaliated by carrying their favourite picnic foods with them when they travel. Tasteful cucumber sandwiches and fresh-fruit delicacies might seem to be acceptable solutions to the current problems, but what about aromatic garlic sausages, overripe goat's cheese and pickled onions? After an hour or so in cramped cabin surroundings these foodstuffs can start to give off strong, unpleasant odours. Since there are no disposal bins in the cabins, passengers tend to stuff leftover food and the wrapping materials into the seat-back literature pockets, which can be the cause of hygiene problems and serious staining. Safety cards, magazines and, in some cases, parts of the seat covers then have to be thrown away.

There has been no indication that there will be cuts in meal services on intercontinental flights. However, there have been several reductions in the overall service: in portion size, menu options and the number of 'go-rounds' by flight attendants. It is ironic that the first-class cabins of some airlines currently have pull-out desk-size tray-tables that are about three times larger than their traditional drop-down predecessors, while at the same time there is a transition to a dining service that is much leaner and meaner than in the past.

### HAUTE CUISINE

The old-style 'dining in the sky' made famous by Pan Am still lives on in the movies and in the hearts and minds of all premium-fare passengers. Even today the arrival of lavishly arrayed aisle carts can signal a memorable communal, interactive experience. In the starring role, the chief flight attendant carves the *filet de boeuf*, carefully extracting rare slices from the middle of the joint and relatively well-done parts from the edges. Assortments of vegetables are presented on large silver salvers, and the 'runner' attendant dashes to the galley for replenishments whenever necessary. The dilemma always seems to be whether to start discreetly at the back row of the cabin and work forward, or to start at the front row and turn the meal service into a gastronomic parade. In the case of ethnic or 'mysterious' food-and-beverage presentations – for example the Arabic-style coffee service, *rijsttafel* (Indonesian rice dishes), toad-in-the-hole (sausages baked in batter) and *feijoada* (Brazilian black beans) – many passengers say that they enjoy watching the rituals associated with the serving process.

In the first-class cabins of some international airlines, the introduction of lie-flat sleeper beds in chevron format has put an end to the elegant trolley service and the gastronomic glories of yesteryear; there is no longer sufficient suitable space for the old-style trolleys. Today there is a far greater emphasis on serving food that has been pre-plated and can be presented directly to individual passengers. In order to demonstrate their commitment to putting the customer first, many airlines are dispensing with fixed times for the meal service, offering instead such alternatives as 'Eat-When-You-Like', 'Sky Snacks', 'Raid the Larder', 'Express Meal', 'Executive Options', 'All-Day-Deli' and 'Quick Cuisine'. At Virgin Atlantic, the Upper Class 'Freedom' menu states unequivocally: 'Treat this service as though you are in a restaurant. Order

Courtesy Iberia

what you want when you want. Our cabin crew will let you know the latest ordering time for hot food.'

The trend toward this type of service means that the menu options have to be capable of being reheated, bistro style, at any time during the flight, as opposed to the traditional cooking process where a particular combination of food items – parboiled or otherwise – was brought to a collective 'ready status' at a defined time. Single-portion servings of pub food, pies, pizzas and pastas are becoming very popular, even in the premium cabins. Some flight attendants say that the on-board atmosphere is now closer to that of a fast-food deli than to that of an exclusive restaurant, and that their work programmes, consequently, have become less predictable.

To make a grand statement, airlines occasionally fly 'on-board chefs', or they might arrange for a chef from the flight kitchen to circulate in the premium cabins prior to take off or in the VIP airport lounges when passengers are waiting to board the aircraft. The aim is to acquaint passengers with the menu of the day, and to explain the range of house wines on offer. The white toque can

have a miraculous effect on even the most dyspeptic traveller.

To add distinction to their menu presentations, airlines proudly display their relationships with celebrity restaurateurs – for example the Chefs' Conclave, the Masters of the Culinary Art, the Congress of Chefs, the International Association of Culinary Professionals and La Confrérie de la Chaîne des Rôtisseurs.

## CUISINE MINCEUR

A welcome development in recent years has been the greater emphasis on lighter, more healthy dining, with the increased use of fresh in-season ingredients. The number and size of the portions tend to be smaller, and food is more often presented in vertical arrangements whereby the thrifty provisioning is disguised as part of an artistic display on smaller plates. On some airlines, low-calorie, low-sodium, low-cholesterol and vegetarian dishes are now available as standard menu choices, and do not have to be ordered in advance as special dietary requirements.

At Air Canada, at the beginning of the 1990s, there was an early pioneering programme in Classe Affaires (executive class),

The menu stated that the new dining programme had been verified and approved according to nutritional specifications: NutriCuisine was designed to offer ' . . . our Executive travellers more nutritionally balanced dishes controlled in specific nutrients essential to their lifestyle'. In recent years, all major airlines have developed health-food options. For example, Delta's Business Elite Menu offers 'Mentally Tough Ideal Performance Meals'. A star by an entry on the menu indicates: 'If you plan to work on board . . . these meals will keep you alert now and allow you to rest upon landing.' Dishes include sliced salmon gravlax, Asian-style beef tenderloin, grilled marinated Mexican snapper and fresh fruit. A plus sign indicates: 'If you have an important meeting on arrival . . . these choices will help you to rest on board and be alert upon arrival.' Options here include vegetable pinwheel spinach wrap, spring mix salad, vegetarian pasta, satisfying soup, raspberry poached pears, and savoury caramelized onion and smoked Gouda cheese omelette.

## TABLEWARE

On-board crockery and cutlery are becoming progressively more functional and more resilient, with high-tech materials now in everyday use. Multipurpose containers have to be stackable, to make the best use of scarce galley storage space, particularly on very long flights that cater multiple meals. For stemware, the centre of gravity is gradually getting closer to the tabletop: tall, thin wineglasses are being phased out in favour of more compact shapes. And teacups and saucers are being superseded by easy-to-handle and easy-to-wash mugs and beakers.

Following the 11 September 2001 terrorist attacks, for security reasons many airlines stopped carrying implements such as ice picks and carving knives. They have also withdrawn all metal knives and forks, and are now flying plastic cutlery in all classes of service. Even in many gate lounge hospitality areas plastic cutlery is now the norm. There is, however, an argument in favour of issuing metal steak knives to all adult passengers at the time of boarding: would potential hijackers with box-cutter blades dare to attack a crew member if they knew that large groups of passengers could, in a crisis situation, use their knives to fight back in a concerted way? Long used in the economy-class cabin, plastic knives and forks are reasonably practical when the food has been shredded or ground, or pre-cut into chunks, or when a piece of meat is relatively over-cooked. But for solid pieces of meat served underdone a plastic knife is unlikely to be an efficient tool, and this could therefore lead to an increase in the portion throwaway rate – a statistic that food-and-beverage departments monitor in great detail.

## PRESENTATION

The gurus of the business still favour white as the best background colour for the presentation of food, as is the case at virtually all the best restaurants. Individual identity can be displayed via insignia markings, or coloured bands, set subtly around the edges of the plates. Traditionally, national flag-carrier airlines have flown proprietary table settings that they have designed in conjunction with prominent, home-based companies; for example British

Courtesy China Southern

*In the air, as on the ground, fast-food service gained greatly in popularity during the 1990s. Once associated with hungry, on-the-move teenagers, individual portions of reheatable pies, pizzas and pastas can be handed to passengers of any age-group and in any class of service whenever they are feeling peckish (as described in Chapter 1/First-Class Luxury*

Courtesy Emirates

*RIGHT: All airline flight kitchens mandate strict supervision of the handling of food and the preparation of in-flight meals. Hygiene standards have to be meticulously observed from the time of purchasing produce and individual ingredients to the end of the process when garbage has to be disposed of and physically removed from the premises within a defined time-scale. Every stage of the critical path has to be actively supervised by qualified chefs*

Airways uses Royal Doulton and Wedgwood china. However, many airlines look to international multi-sourcing to achieve significant cost savings. Bob Bregman, President of WESSCO International, a leading supplier of customized import products to the airline industry, explains: 'We have specialized in supplying custom airline tableware for over 20 years. In particular, the quality of "Made in China" tableware has improved so greatly over the last decade that some of the world's top proprietary brands have even moved some of their production there. We maintain our own branch office in China.'

To further offset their dollar outlay, some airlines run tie-in marketing campaigns with famous-brand makers of, say, the coffee and ice cream that are served on board. Marketing messages can be incorporated into the dining experience – on menu inserts, cocktail napkins and meal trays. Edward Gargano, President and CEO of MHM North America, describes how airlines can capitalize on non-performing assets by making tray-tables work for their living: 'Using vinyl decals, revenue-producing advertising can be affixed to the inner side of the drop-down tray-table. Based on actual head counts of the captive audience, this kind of programme can deliver a steady monthly income.'

These days, the romance with jet-set dining is fading rapidly, and cost-cutting and convenience food are now the norm in economy class. Ryanair sells wrapped sandwiches during flights, and at some airports local entrepreneurs sell 'boarding-gate bags', which contain meals priced at different levels. Purists might argue that this approach hardly represents the spirit of hospitality; but for a family group travelling in economy class, after two hours or more spent queuing at check-in and security points, and after having already spent three hours or more getting from home to the airport, these rough-and-ready solutions might be the equivalent of a godsend.

## INTERNATIONAL GOURMET DINING

On the prestige long-haul airlines, however, the grand tradition continues. At Japan Airlines, Alan Ogawa, Vice President, Airport Operations, the Americas, says: 'We did not cut back our food-and-beverage service in any way following 11 September 2001. At all times we have continued to offer our full menu service. We offer both Japanese and Western cuisine, and we provide delicacies that are specific to certain geographical areas. For example, on our Tokyo–Singapore route, for breakfast we serve *congee*, a rice porridge, which many of our passengers like to eat with pickles, and special condiments.'

But how is the demand calculated? Ogawa continues: 'There are established patterns for the ratio of Western to Oriental food, and each station that is responsible for providing advance meal counts has its own formula for tracking the information. We are constantly trying to minimize the expense of "lost meals" – currently it stands at some 3 per cent. At all our turn-point stations, our flight kitchens load fresh food. We have to be able to control the hygiene standards, of course.'

And planning the menus? 'Japan Airlines has subsidiary catering companies at many of its major stations. At other stations we entrust catering services to contracted vendors. We run four menu cycles per year – our "Seasons Programme". The table linens, headrest covers and menus are coordinated with the colours and tastes associated with the changing seasons.'

But how does the airline achieve product differentiation? 'In the first-class cabin the service is ultra-luxurious; there are several meal options, including caviar,' explains Ogawa. 'In the business-class cabin we have a service called "Amuse Bouche" – unusual and special canapés served with the cocktails. After their starter course, passengers are offered a choice between two Western

Courtesy China Southern

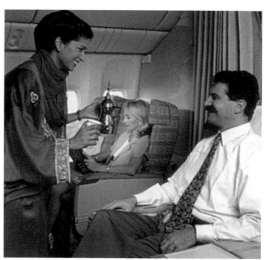
Courtesy Emirates

Courtesy Japan Airlines

*RIGHT: The ultimate in movie-style luxury: the traditional first-class aisle-trolley service. Passengers are served individually, and the available gastronomic glories can range from caviar, lobster and freshly sliced beef to iced fruit and handmade confectionery (the way in which Japan Airlines manages this complex process is described in this Chapter)*

Courtesy Japan Airlines

Courtesy Mexicana

LEFT: The top international airlines have to cater to the tastes of passengers from all parts of the world, who are accustomed to the finest restaurant and hotel dining services. To delight the eye and brain before engaging the palate demands perfection in presentation

dishes – which could be either beef, fish or chicken – and one Japanese dish.'

And how does the airline keep up with the latest trends? 'We run our research internally, but we also have a consultation process that involves the Japan Escoffier Association and several well-known chefs from top hotels, for example the Okura, the Prince and the Imperial in Tokyo.'

Looking ahead to the increased stage lengths and the huge passenger loads planned for the powerful aircraft of the future, it is clear that the food-and-beverage arrangements will require imaginative and meticulous handling. To paraphrase the immortal words of Lord Lytton, the English poet and statesman and Viceroy of India (1876–80):

We may live without love – what is passion but pining?
But where are the folks who can live without dining?
We may live without friends, we may live without books,
But civilized folks cannot live without cooks.

## COMMENTS FROM THE SPECIALISTS

### Owen Graham Jullies

*Food and Beverage Manager, Product Planning, South African Airways*

As operators of one of the world's ultra-long flight segments – New York–Johannesburg – South African Airways attempts to make the dining experience pleasant and fulfilling in what can be a 15-hour marathon. Passengers range from those who are ravenous to those who simply want to sleep for the entire trip.

Leaving New York in the early evening, we offer a full dinner service appropriate to the local departure time. However, nearing arrival in South Africa a full breakfast is served although the local time is midday. The cabin shades are kept closed to maintain an early-morning environment, and there is no disruption of the passenger's internal time clock. Between meals, we also have

programmes for mild exercise and appropriate liquid intake. In fact, we have noticed a decline in liquor consumption on intercontinental flights as people have become more aware of health issues.

Sensitivity to the cabin environment is even apparent in how South African selects its on-board wines. To promote local products, a panel of 12 judges (six South African and six international) select from more than 700 local varieties. The airline briefs the judges on the effects of high-altitude long-haul cabin conditions so that this information can be applied to the final selections.

### John Varley

*General Manager UK, Meridiana SpA*

As with every other airline, we have had to rethink the approach to in-flight dining. Traditionally, on a two-hour flight Meridiana serves a choice of one hot meal or an attractive cold entrée in first class, and a single cold plate in economy. We are still maintaining the service in first class, complete with ovens and service from a cart.

In economy we are moving to a more modest presentation, as has most of the industry. Whereas previously all meals were catered and boarded locally, for cost reasons, we are seeing a trend to full catering at our main base in Italy. This works well unless there are delays, and then it can be difficult to maintain a fresh look and taste in a meal that is served several hours after it was scheduled to be eaten.

### Susan Henry

*Managing Director, Onboard Services and Catering, Northwest Airlines*

Northwest's route structure gives us the opportunity to serve multiple markets, in terms of domestic and long-haul international flights, variety of passenger types and customer expectations. The challenge to dining services is to take into account these varied demands and to do it in a manner that is cost efficient and consistent in terms of delivery.

Courtesy China Southern

Courtesy China Southern

Courtesy China Southern

# Chapter 7
## REAL-FEEL CUSTOMER TOUCHPOINTS

*How often do airlines physically 'touch' their customers? Even the minor miscellaneous items (MMIs) can have a major impact. How should vendors and suppliers approach this subject?*

**POINTS OF CONTACT**

In the US alone there are more than 30,000 flights daily. So imagine the thousands or, depending upon passenger loads, millions of moments when customers are physically in contact with an airline; that is, touching some element of the cabin interior. On the occasion of each and every contact, the airline has an opportunity to make a great impression – for better or for worse. Many of the obvious contact areas are already fixed in position inside the aircraft. Following are some typical 'touchpoints':

- at the entryway – the doormat, doorframe, hard floor covering, wall-panel coverings, carpet, bump strip (a surface-mounted protective covering in heavy-duty plastic or vinyl) and kick strip (a heavy-duty plastic covering installed from the floorboards up to ankle level to protect areas likely to suffer from being kicked);
- at the seat position – the seat-cover fabric, headrest area, seat safety belt and buckle, mandatory placards, the safety cards, armrests, legrest, footrest, recline mechanism, dado panel, tray-table, literature pocket, switches and buttons of the passenger service unit

(PSU), the controls of the in-flight entertainment system, power-supply outlet, in-seat telephone, headset, TV, individual reading light, handles of the window shades and the latch of the overhead stowage bin;

- in the lavatory – the door handle, door lock, toilet seat, safety grab bar, toilet-paper dispenser, the flush handle, taps, soap dispenser, hand-towel dispenser, paper-cup holders and the racks of toiletries.

The major elements of a cabin interior-design scheme, for example the carpets, wall coverings and the fabrics used for curtains and seat covers, have to meet rigorous certification requirements. By contrast, however, a large number of potential touchpoints are classed as minor miscellaneous items (MMIs): as such, the standards and design details for accessories such as headrest covers, blankets, cushions, in-flight literature, entertainment guides, children's play kits and cocktail napkins are controlled in-house by the airlines themselves. Obviously, good hygiene and the very highest safety standards are a must for all personal-contact items on board an aircraft, and in particular the blankets and pillows need special attention to ensure that they meet fire-safety requirements.

Courtesy China Southern

Courtesy United

Courtesy Qantas

When surveying the cabin interior, customers tend to regard the design scheme as a 'given' – they might remark that it looks very modern or colourful, or quiet or dramatic, for example. However, their reactions to small, individual items vary and, because of the physical process of touching, holding, handling and smelling, opinions are likely to be much more personal. Battered safety cards or dirty coat hangers do not engender feelings of confidence, while sparkly clean linen can make everyone feel relaxed and pampered. After the flight, when passengers make assessments of the quality of the airline, their analysis is rarely based purely on rationale; they are also influenced by their feelings and gut reactions. It is likely that, on a long trip, the memory of down-filled duvets, fluffy pillows and comfortable sleeping suits will contribute more to passenger satisfaction levels than all the colours and patterns of the carpets, curtains and wall coverings put together.

### The importance of MMIs

If handled well, the MMI budget can help to achieve a high level of distinctiveness and memorability, directly linked to the product-planning platforms. If the airline so chooses, the MMI programme can be used to display ethnic, cultural or fashion statements, or practical marketing messages. For example, images of local flora and fauna can be incorporated into the patterns on fabrics used for such items as headrest and cushion covers; foil-covered chocolate medallions can be distributed to celebrate local festive occasions; menu covers and inserts can announce new routes and services or marketing tie-in agreements; the airline's frequent-flyer organization can use on-board brochures to sign up new members; and unique identity markings can be placed on cabin bag-tags. In addition, passengers appreciate some of the relatively more humble accessories, including:

- cocktail stir-sticks sporting the emblem of the airline;
- paper cocktail napkins displaying welcome messages;
- decorative 'banding' wrapped around small items;
- in-flight literature showing pictures of the fleet and the related cabin layouts;
- drinks coasters displaying greetings in foreign languages;
- certificates signed by the flight-deck crew;
- maps showing the flight plan; and
- lapel badges, tiepins and clip-on pilots' wings showing airline logo markings.

## TOUCHING MOMENTS

To create a pleasing and elegant presentation, all touchpoints need to be carefully coordinated, not just with the fixed elements of the cabin interior-design installations but also with those articles that are boarded and stowed before take off, and which make their appearance at appointed times during the flight.

### The food-and-beverage service

This includes trays; tray liners; menus; serving plates; bowls, cups and saucers; knives, forks and spoons; glasses; sachets and packets containing nuts, pretzels, salt, pepper, sauce, salad dressing, sugar, sweetener and powdered milk; toothpicks; dining napkins and the accompanying hand towels.

### As-needed articles

These include motion-sickness bags, baby bassinets, magazine folders, duty-free catalogues, the 'Do Not Disturb' and 'Wake for Breakfast' adhesive labels, and playing cards.

### Hospitality baskets

Flight attendants move through the cabin at intervals carrying baskets from which passengers can choose from an assortment of goodies such as candies, chocolate bars, iced lollipops, fruit and freshly baked cookies, or personal items such as perfumed towelettes, buttonhole flowers, hair combs, nail files, mouthwash and so on.

Courtesy South African Airways

Courtesy Qantas

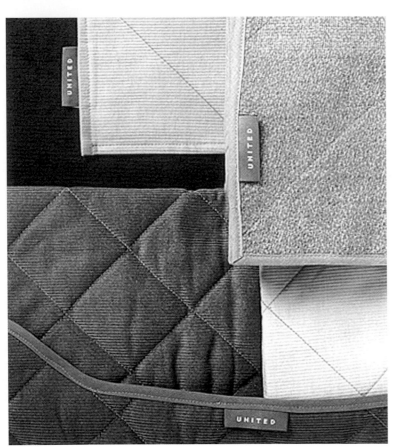

Courtesy United

*An airline can make a distinctive impression through its handling of details. Because paying passengers do not like to be regarded as a captive advertising audience, it is preferable to position airline names in a discreet, elegant way – as shown on the carry-on cabin baggage bag-tags (above, right). From the passengers' point of view, the reference to the prestigious first-class or business-class cabin is extremely important and this information is frequently presented in a more bold way. The stitched-in identity markings (shown on the left) are similar to those that appear on pricey designer-label garments and high-end household goods. In the aviation world they can serve a practical purpose, acting as security tags during the cycles of washing and dry cleaning and when these items are positioned in a storage facility in the vicinity of other, similar items belonging to other airlines*

## Sample boxes

In conjunction with local suppliers, some airlines offer small presentation boxes that typically contain personal-care products such as shampoo, toothpaste and skin lotion. According to Richard Bogash, Managing Director, Sky Marketing Services, LLC: 'Over the last few years, a number of marketers of branded products have formed partnerships with airlines to help promote their products. This marketing technique is viewed as a positive in-flight programme for the airline, the passenger and the consumer product company, by providing products with a widely branded appeal at no cost to the airline. The carrier has the opportunity to present to its non-premium passengers either a package of travel-related compatible items or individual items. The most common form of distribution is placement on the meal tray, in a snack pack, or individually distributed by the flight attendants. Because the passengers in economy class do not normally receive amenity kits, the sample boxes help to provide a value-added image of the airline.'

## Amenity kits

These might contain an eye mask, slipper socks, earplugs, a hair brush, a nail file, hand cream, cosmetics, a razor, shaving cream, a shoe-polishing sponge, mouthwash, a toothbrush and toothpaste. For long-haul carriers this is a very competitive area. Some airlines offer elegant leather and suede pouches that can subsequently be used as fashion accessories or to store jewellery or precious objects. Other airlines offer practical zip-up boxes made of plastic or fabric, which can later be used to store CDs. Over the years there have been various fads, including drawstring bags, belt pouches, all-purpose sports-style holders with Velcro or stud fasteners, and a range of containers resembling biscuit tins. In general, the amenity-kit holder is a vehicle for presenting the identity markings of the individual airline. Traditionally it has been classed as a collectible item along with sleeping suits, slippers, printed menu cards and signed certificates from the flight deck.

*This small slip-on bag-tag communicates at a number of different levels. In addition to the insignia and house colours of the airline, the graphic display includes the website address (for flight and fare information) and the SkyTeam seal or 'hallmark', which denotes Alliance partnership status (as described in Chapter 4/Aero Identity)*

Courtesy Qantas

Courtesy Pan Am/George Design Studio

*Although of an inherently disposable nature, on-board amenity items often become treasured as 'collectibles', not just by the airline passengers, but by their family members, neighbours and local schoolchildren*

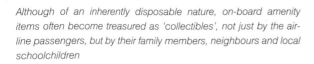

## Give-away items

Seasoned air travellers still talk about one of the gifts offered by KLM in the early days of mass air travel: the charming blue-and-white Dutch porcelain houses that were filled with alcohol. More common these days are executive-style accessories such as key cases, luggage tags, diaries, address books, pens, paperweights, bookmarks and writing materials. Anything bearing a Concorde logo is likely to become a treasured memento. Other sought-after items include CDs of the music associated with the country where the carrier is based, local postcards, stamps and guidebooks. Increasingly, these gift programmes are partly funded by the national tourist authority. Gifts that are compact and lightweight are easier for passengers to carry off the aircraft: large pictures, vases, costume dolls and document portfolios are difficult to tuck into carry-on baggage. Inevitably, some of these items get left behind, are swept up after the flight by the local cleaning crews, and do not therefore represent a good use of the airline budget!

Jeff Ruffolo, Public Relations Manager at China Southern Airlines, explains his company's philosophy: 'In addition to the normal range of amenities that we carry on board our aircraft, we offer specially made gifts to our "Premium Business" customers, for example Chinese belts and wallets in fine leather, ties and clocks. These are presented on a silver tray by the flight attendants shortly after passenger embarkation. The airline is extremely proud of its ethnic heritage: our gifts are exclusive to China Southern and carry the insignia of the airline.'

## TOUCHING THE SENSES

In their jetliner cabins airlines have innumerable opportunities to make passengers feel happy or unhappy. But it is not always easy to predict reactions to new sensory experiences, for example, during the 1990s it was fashionable on some US airlines to bake cookies in the galleys to be served with tea, coffee or milk shortly prior to landing. Some passengers loved waking up to the scent of the wafting aromas but others did not. (It is tempting to wonder whether in future decades there might be a move toward organizing on-board perfume programmes – whiffs of mountain breezes or summer meadows could be time-controlled and co-ordinated with the overall flight routing!)

Public address systems need to work efficiently and crew members need to be trained to make clear announcements. Passengers are bound to worry if they think that they may have misheard something important. Taped music played during the enplaning and deplaning processes needs to be carefully selected to help provide a welcoming ambience.

To ensure ease of readability of on-board printed material (for example safety cards, menus, instructions for using the telephone or the TV set) it is necessary to take into account the typical lighting conditions. Colour choices, type-faces and letter sizes can be calibrated to provide the maximum level of clarity, in order to help passengers feel confident about their ability to absorb this flow of information throughout the entire air journey.

*Above: Pictograms can help provide useful information for polyglot passenger groups on international flights. Yes, a picture can be worth a thousand words! Left: A souvenir kangaroo lapel pin from Qantas, the letters of which stand for Queensland and Northern Territory Aerial Service*

Courtesy South African Airways

*The professional touch: the memory of the 'feel' of an aircraft lives on long after the flight has ended!*

Courtesy China Southern

## TACTILE VALUES

In terms of making a good impression on both customers and employees, it helps if the style, colour and finish of all the small items that appear in sequence during the flight can be smoothly coordinated with those of the larger, more costly elements of the cabin interior scheme. When considered individually, each moment of contact might seem relatively unimportant. But if all the touchpoints are added together this generates a revealing picture of direct customer experience – a subject that warrants serious study by the marketing specialists.

'At Singapore Airlines, our goal in passenger service is to actively find ways to create a more satisfied customer,' says James Boyd, Public Relations Director for the Americas. 'Our strategy is to base our product development on "themes" of emotive content to enhance the experience on board our aircraft. Connectivity is one theme that we use in the cabin to maintain the environment that most of our passengers have on the ground. We pioneered the facility to allow email transmissions from the passenger seat, and

telephone access from any seat position to any telephone in the world. This theme is currently being extended to users of laptop computers: in business class, we are converting from standard DC power to AC outlets so that a passenger can plug in – as on the ground – and forget how long the battery will operate.

'We focus on passenger control of the environment. Most of our customers are used to being in control, but traditionally most airlines have dictated when a passenger eats, sleeps and is entertained on board an aircraft. Singapore Airlines offers pre-departure menus, which allow first-class and business-class passengers to select from more than 17 different entrées up to 24 hours before departure. The on-board entertainment is a server-based fibre-optic system, which allows the passenger to create an individual 12-track programme from more than 140 stored options.

'On the ground, in our first- and business-class lounges, we extend both of these themes to the transit and pre-departure period. The lounges do not copy our aircraft interior-design schemes, but they do use the same warm, subtle and muted approach to colour, combined with heavy staff support. For example, in addition to Internet access and a full bar at the Narita Silver Kris lounge, we offer up to a week's back issues of *The Straits Times* (so that passengers can catch up with what's been going on) and Ben & Jerry's ice-cream samples to allow North American passengers to feel closer to home.'

## FINE TUNING, CLOSE HARMONY

In the field of architecture it is said that 'God is in the details'. In aviation, however, the great airlines are the ones that handle details successfully, whether operationally or within the passenger cabin. Of course, it is true that for the logistics and purchasing departments the provisioning of MMIs can rapidly turn into a nightmare, for example, the tales of menus written specifically for the Asian markets turning up (mysteriously) on the South American routes! All airlines, vendors and suppliers can aim to raise passenger perception levels by giving careful consideration to the running of their MMI and associated touchpoint programmes.

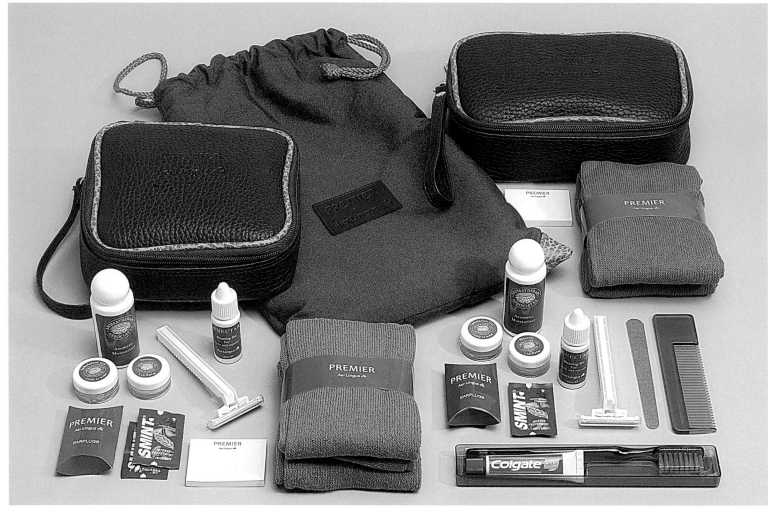

Courtesy Aer Lingus

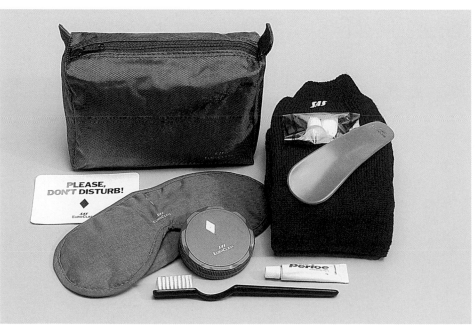

Courtesy SAS

## COMMENTS FROM THE SPECIALISTS

### Daniel Baron
*Asia-Pacific Editor, Aircraft Interiors magazine*

In the microcosm of the aircraft cabin, more often than not we are surrounded by touchpoints but are still left feeling untouched. What's missing? Sense of humour. Eagerness to please all audiences equally, or fear that the carrier will be perceived as lacking interest in safety, results in that most contemptible of afflictions: lowest-common-denominator syndrome. But dumbing down the experience is a foolproof recipe for an excruciatingly bland brand. Which is why those airlines that do add a bit of humour really stand out.

One of them is SAS. Inviting phrases such as 'Off we go!' appear outside, adjacent to the forward door, to greet boarding passengers. And whimsical sayings on salt and pepper packets (for example, 'Imagine if the oceans contained pepper instead of salt. Well . . . maybe not') both put a smile on the customer's face at that moment and serve as a small yet lasting reminder of the essence of the SAS brand.

Another winner with a sense of humour is Virgin Atlantic. In the pre–11 September 2001 days, the airline's stylish Upper Class cutlery was a bit too popular, performing a regular vanishing act. So Virgin came up with the clever idea of putting 'Stolen from Virgin Atlantic' on the back of its silverware. The carrier created a tongue-in-cheek touchpoint, leveraging theft into an advertising gimmick.

Airlines should also look to incorporate touchpoints in the lavatory, a space that was overlooked for decades. On Cathay Pacific we now find coloured tiles on the floor, and on All Nippon Airways blue-glass sinks. Japanese airlines are to be applauded for their 'dressing steps', panels for changing clothes that fold down from the lavatory wall to rest just above the floor. Some airlines add a nice touch with fresh flowers in their lavatories.

Equally impressive is the ever-evolving amenity kit, with its lotions and potions carrying names like D-Stress and Temple Spa. Both the kits and their contents are touchpoints that cleverly appeal to our longing for a bit of time alone to exhale, contemplate and reflect.

### Peter Sheahan
*Sheahan & Associates, Scarsdale, New York*

It is interesting to look at the ways in which aircraft interior touchpoints can be linked with activities in the outside world. For example, in 2001 Thai International introduced a new series of souvenirs that included Thai silk and other products from the SUPPORT Foundation, which is under the patronage of Her Majesty Queen Sirikit of Thailand.

The launch announcement stated: 'Passengers travelling on all intercontinental routes will receive on-board souvenirs produced by Her Majesty's SUPPORT Foundation. These are made of Thai silk and cotton. This is part of Thai's policy to help promote and support Thai products – and especially Thai silk – that are made and created by Thai people. Passengers will find them both beautiful and useful, while gaining satisfaction from the knowledge that they are also helping create job opportunities and additional earnings for people living in rural areas.'

The suit hangers and bags made from silk and cotton were given to Royal First and Royal Executive Class passengers travelling on board Thai flights of four hours or more, originating in Bangkok and bound for destinations in Europe and the United States, as well as in Australia, China and Japan.

Organizing small gestures of goodwill through programmes such as aircraft interior touchpoints can help people feel good about themselves and the world around them.

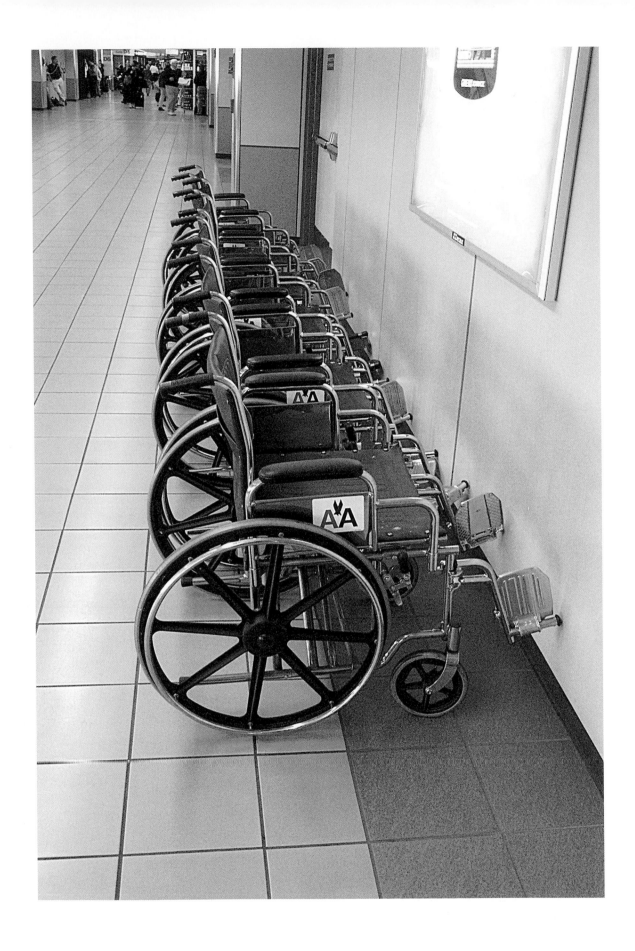

# Chapter 8
## ACCESSIBILITY
Special Needs

*How can air travel be made more comfortable for a growing class of passengers with special needs?*

For families travelling with small children, overcrowded and frenetic check-in and security lines can constitute a hostile environment. What is being done to develop child-friendly approaches to the air travel experience? And for elderly travellers and those with disabilities, a journey by air can be a miserable experience – the difficulties seem to be never-ending. How many airports or airlines have policy codes, disability units or training material relating to passengers who require special help and consideration?

In the United States, since the passing of the Americans with Disabilities Act (ADA) in 1990, there have been great improvements – across the manufacturing, industrial and service sectors – in accessibility, space allowances, reach ranges and special facilities for use by people with disabilities. In public areas, and in recently constructed buildings, installations now generally include:

- passageways and lobbies that can accommodate the turning radius of wheelchairs;
- handrails and safety grab bars on staircases and in corridors;
- doorways that open and close automatically;
- curbside ramps that provide safe access;
- water coolers and drinking fountains at wheelchair height;
- specially equipped toilets, bath tubs and shower stalls;
- signs displaying internationally recognized symbols;
- reserved seating areas near doorways and entrance and exit routes; and
- specially configured platform lifts and elevators.

In addition, special vehicle registration plates are available that designate the status of drivers with disabilities, and there are allocated car-parking spaces. New requirements call for routes to be suitably illuminated; for work-surface heights and clearances to be

Courtesy Medline Industries Inc.

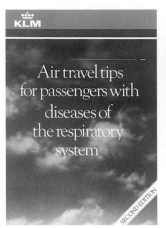

As with walking frames, wheelchairs need to be sufficiently sturdy for use by fully grown adults. Transportation to and from the door of the aircraft or airport terminal buildings requires strong, serviceable equipment (as shown in this Chapter)

Courtesy Junkin Safety

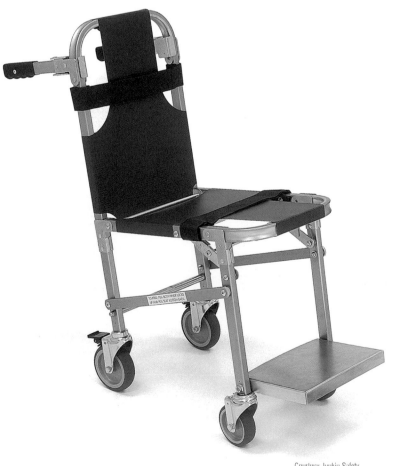

Courtesy Junkin Safety

adjusted according to individual needs, and for 'trip' hazards such as toe-catching projecting overhangs to be eliminated from staircase steps and saddle thresholds (surface-mounted divider strips covering the joins or tiny gaps at doorways).

However, despite the regulatory requirements of the ADA, and the provisions of the Air Carrier Access Act, in the field of air travel the level of dissatisfaction in this area continues to rise. At the end of the last millennium, at the US Department of Transportation, there was an amazing 81 per cent increase in the number of complaints from people with disabilities alleging air-travel discrimination, and airlines were faced with the possibility of major fines because of their lack of service for these passengers. Main complaints included the failure of airlines to provide wheelchairs as required by law; long waits for wheelchairs; passengers being stranded inside aircraft for extended periods; and even being left at the wrong gate, resulting in missed flights.

However, the European Commission and the 28 member companies of the Association of European Airlines have recently announced a new Code of Conduct. The provisions include a commitment to 'help handicapped passengers' and 'to improve assistance to passengers in difficulty', the overall aim, according to the Commissioner for Transport, Loyola de Palacio, being 'to change the impression felt by many air passengers that they have been abandoned.'

A number of airlines have already taken significant steps in this direction. At Continental, Vern Alg, Senior Manager, Interiors Engineering, explains: 'In the mid-1990s we set up an inter-departmental task force to address this issue. Continental recognized that there are, in fact, many customers with disabilities. Although some of the commonly encountered disabilities are clearly visible, many are not so visible. We set out to identify ways in which we can work with all these customers. We see this as our social responsibility. We have developed a range of special training material, website information and brochures. From the initial inquiry, the details relating to the individual passenger are noted in the Passenger Name Registration (PNR), the computer reservation entry. On board our aircraft we carry special aisle-size wheelchairs equipped with "slider boards" so that a customer can transfer with the minimum of discomfort from one seat position to another. All our flight attendants receive training in how to care for passengers with disabilities.'

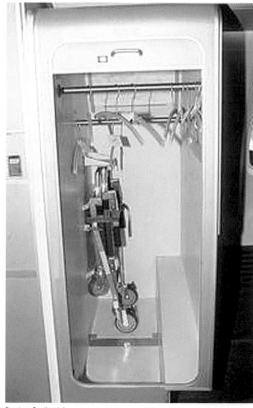

Courtesy Continental

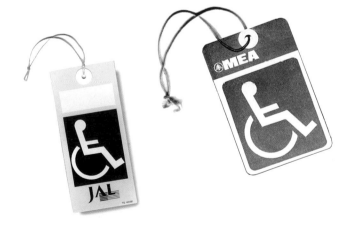

*Special aisle-size wheelchairs designed and approved for use on board aircraft can be folded (opposite) and stowed in the cabin inside a coat closet (see left)*

## PROBLEMS IN THE AIR

In product surveys, mobility-impaired passengers have always complained about aircraft lavatories. Following are some typical comments:

- 'There are never enough lavatories for the number of passengers on the aircraft.'
- 'The lavatories on board are even worse than the ones at the airport.'
- 'They're always too small.'
- 'You need to be a contortionist to get in and out of them.'
- 'I always hit my head on those dreadful curved ceilings.'
- 'Why do they put grab bars at shoulder level, instead of where you need them, when you're actually using the toilet?'
- 'Trying to get back to your seat in the dark is a nightmare. The floor surfaces can be so uneven, with ridges and bumps in the hard bits of linoleum, and carpet that feels like chewing gum. There's never anything for me to hang on to when I walk past the galleys and closets.'

With careful thought and application, the on-board environment can be made far less hostile. Describing the new wide-body aircraft at Continental, Vern Alg emphasizes: 'There is one larger rest room that is wheelchair accessible on all wide-body aircraft. All rest rooms are equipped with extra grab bars. As usual, the doors of the rest room can, in an emergency, be removed, even when locked on the inside. On each narrow-body aircraft, we have one designated rest room that has vanity curtains fore and aft – to provide privacy for anyone who needs to leave the door open (for example when being assisted by a personal attendant). On all our new aisle-side seats, there is a latch that flight attendants can use to flip up the armrest to facilitate access to the seat row.'

Passengers using arm or elbow crutches also have special requirements, for example what happens during the boarding process? For reasons of safety, the crutch needs to be stowed in a suitable location. On aircraft that have large overhead bins for passengers' carry-on baggage, it is usually possible for the flight attendant to stow the crutch close to its owner. However, on aircraft that have small bins it might be necessary for the flight attendant to stow the crutch in a coat closet, possibly at the other end of the aircraft. In this case, at the time of disembarkation the same flight attendant should not forget to retrieve the crutch. If the flight attendant is busy elsewhere, the passenger will have a hard time trying to explain to a completely new face that though the crutch is somewhere on the aircraft, its precise location is unknown, and that without it he or she will simply not be able to get up and leave the aircraft.

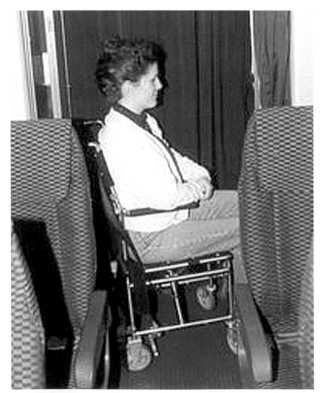

Courtesy Continental

Courtesy Continental

*The armrests of some of the newer-model aisle-side seats can be raised to help passengers with disabilities to gain access to their seat rows more easily*

## ON THE GROUND

At transition points, passengers with disabilities complain of a host of difficulties:

- wheelchairs are often undersized, flimsy or, worse, dangerously rickety, with missing footplates or faulty brakes;
- moving walkways may not actually move;
- being routed via a maze of bustling retail stores can be unsettling;
- there may be greatly increased distances to departure gates;
- sometimes there is nowhere to sit down in long corridors – the new airport buildings at Shanghai Pudong and Milan Malpensa, for example, are about a mile long;
- lavatories are sometimes located on a different floor from the waiting areas;
- signage can be confusing;
- there is no information on distances – is the walk to passport control 5 minutes or 15?
- employees may be untrained ('I'm not sure how many steps there are to get up to the transit lounge');
- employees are not always helpful ('I don't know – try asking at one of the other desks');

- the local culture is sometimes hostile to travellers whose disabilities are particularly visible;
- there may be long flights of stairs without handrails; and
- at some airports, due to a lack of suitable elevators, passengers with disabilities are still physically (that is, in the arms of two strong helpers) carried up and down flights of steps ('Much faster than going the long way around'), which can be a terrifying experience for everyone.

## HOW TO COPE

To help passengers with disabilities, airlines and airport authorities need to provide kinder, gentler assistance at key transition points: arrival at the curbside, check-in, aircraft boarding and deplaning, baggage collection and transfer to the departure vehicle.

According to Vern Alg of Continental: 'Our baggage handlers are trained to look after wheelchairs. The wheelchairs that we use at Continental have been specially designed for airport use. They are large and sturdy, with a solid wheelbase. If a customer's wheelchair gets damaged during the flight, our baggage-recovery people can provide an immediate substitute and – working through a support network of local suppliers – they can quickly arrange to repair or provide a replacement for the customer's own wheelchair. In the

Courtesy British Airways

*A warm welcome for a four-footed passenger! Nowadays there are special courses to train dogs to become regular fliers, to accompany blind travellers on board aircraft (as explained in this Chapter)*

### AmericanAirlines

| | | |
|---|---|---|
| POINT 'A' | 126 YDS | 378 FT |
| POINT 'D' | 151 YDS | 453 FT |
| POINT 'C' | 181 YDS | 543 FT |
| POINT 'D' | 566 YDS | 1698 FT |
| | | |
| GATE 13 | 640 YDS | 1920 FT |
| GATE 14 | 667 YDS | 2001 FT |
| GATE 15 | 775 YDS | 2325 FT |
| GATE 16 | 586 YDS | 1758 FT |
| GATE 17 | 633 YDS | 1899 FT |
| GATE 18 | 697 YDS | 2091 FT |
| GATE 19 | 717 YDS | 2151 FT |
| GATE 20 | 781 YDS | 2343 FT |
| GATE 21 | 803 YDS | 2409 FT |
| GATE 22 | 861 YDS | 2583 FT |

**WALKING DISTANCES FROM CHECK-IN AREA STAIRS. AVERAGE TIME 20-30 MINUTES.**

PLEASE TAKE TIME TO READ THE INFORMATION ON THIS LEAFLET. IT WILL ASSIST YOU TO ARRIVE AT THE GATE AT LEAST 30 MINS. PRIOR TO DEPARTURE. FAILURE TO DO SO MAY RESULT IN THE REMOVAL OF YOUR BAGGAGE

PTO.

terminal buildings, we strive to provide electric carts that stop at regular pickup points to collect or put down customers who cannot walk the distance to and from the gate lounges.'

From a commercial perspective, if the elderly are grouped with people with disabilities, this represents an enormous and potentially lucrative market segment. Foreseeable growth is guaranteed! Figures from the Organization of Economic Cooperation and Development (OECD) show that, while there were 45 million new retirees per year from 1975 to 2000, this number will rise to 70 million per year from 2000 to 2025. And at the United Nations Second World Assembly on Ageing in 2002 it was stated that a million people now turn 60 every month, that the elderly will soon outnumber the young for the first time in history; and that the number of people over the age of 60 will increase from 600 million in 2002 to a staggering two billion in 2050.

Any airline product-development manager who succeeds in gaining the loyalty of jet-setting pensioners will find that this group can provide a constant flow of revenue. They represent a very flexible market segment with regard to day, date and time of travel. And food and beverage requirements are relatively modest: light, warm, tasty meals, served in small to medium-sized portions. Like young fliers, elderly passengers generally prefer to be seated close to the lavatories. For safety reasons, they should not be seated in the emergency-exit rows.

Good organization is invaluable. At Geneva Airport, for example, there is a designated assembly area for passengers who require special assistance. Local taxi drivers know that they need to use this particular spot for dropping off passengers with disabilities, so that there is only a minimum transit distance across the passenger concourse. And at Bristol Airport, in England, the authorities are working with the organization Guide Dogs for the Blind to improve airport facilities for blind people. With the support of Brymon Airways and British Airways, a new programme has been launched to train suitable dogs to become regular fliers – to accompany blind passengers on board the aircraft.

Courtesy United

Courtesy Boeing

*The illuminated handrail at shoulder height (shown above) can provide an improved level of personal security for passengers with disabilities – and indeed for EVERYONE who walks along the aisle of the aircraft*

## THE FUTURE

Cabin architects might like to ponder the following features on new-generation aircraft:

- the best time to introduce features for passengers with special needs is at the initial design stage;
- there is a clear need to install specially designed lavatories that are suitable for passengers with special needs;
- the forthcoming Airbus A380 promises a lower-lobe toilet area with vanity units, several lavatories and significantly reduced queuing time. But passengers with disabilities will not want to negotiate a staircase. Will they be given a special key to a lavatory located on the main deck?
- for family members travelling together, it is tempting to dream of specially designated play areas inside the new-model long-distance aircraft. But who will be responsible for a group of small children when the aircraft suddenly hits turbulence?
- will there be illuminated handrails that run the length of the passenger cabin? This feature has already been introduced in the Boeing B717 – on the underside of baggage stowage bins, approximately at shoulder height. Passengers and flight attendants alike wonder why this excellent product feature cannot be incorporated into all aircraft types;
- more baby-bassinet positions and oxygen seat positions;

- air-purification systems that will eliminate 100 per cent of airborne germs within the pressurized cabin; the elderly and the very young are especially vulnerable to infection;
- in-flight medical services, via telephone contact and computer tracking systems;
- and, just maybe, meal tray-tables that do not require double-jointed elbows for their deployment!

Finally, if the definition of passengers with disabilities is further extended to include anyone who is less than 100 per cent fit, it has to be assumed that at some point all members of the flying populace will come within that scope. Whether a passenger is suffering from a headache, a toothache, a bad back, an upset stomach, a temper tantrum or just plain old age, every one of us will eventually need a little extra help.

At one level, this topic is an appeal to conscience, a moral imperative. At another level, however, it calls attention to the need to keep abreast of the times by ensuring customer satisfaction. When planning their work programmes for the aviation sector, architects, designers, manufacturers, vendors and suppliers will be able to guarantee a greatly enhanced customer base for their products and services if they keep in mind the special needs of their passengers in what has become an increasingly challenging market segment.

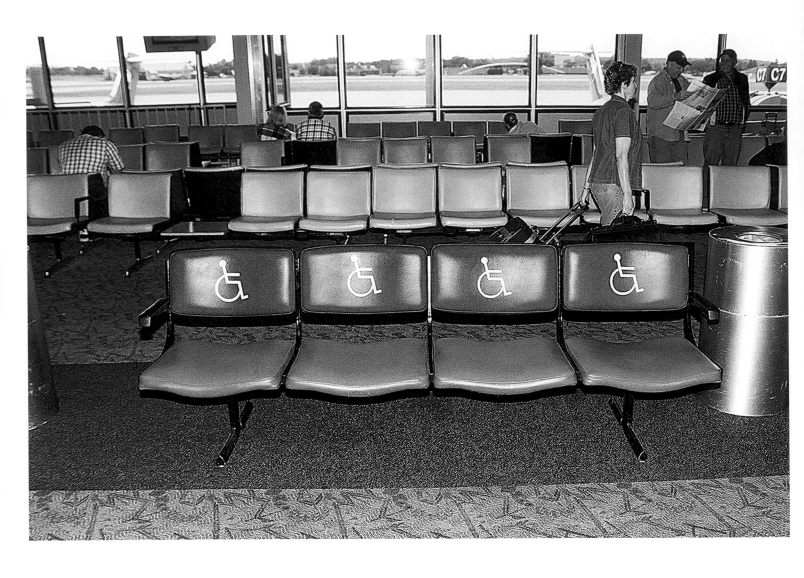

The most important requirement for passengers with special needs is assistance provided by attendants who have been properly trained. Grudging or clumsily enthusiastic help can create problems for everyone

## COMMENTS FROM THE SPECIALISTS

### David Weiner
*Architect, New York*

With the passage of the Americans with Disabilities Act (ADA) in 1990, the US Government required that all public facilities be accessible to people with disabilities. This new regulation was not simply a matter of tailoring and adjusting local building codes to provide wheelchair access; it was a wide, sweeping piece of civil-rights legislation acknowledging accessibility and access as a social right for all people, regardless of their disability.

The consequences of this new legislation have affected almost every business and industry. Aside from the obvious need for public buildings to be made accessible, a number of previously overlooked issues have now come to the forefront of design modification. Specifically, the public-transportation sector is an evolving area adjusting itself to the myriad complications for its users with disabilities. For example, subways are not only having to provide elevators down to platforms but are also planning ways for people with sight and hearing impairments to navigate the systems. Bus and rail systems are similarly affected and are making adjustments to the entire sequence of circulation movement, from car drop-off points at stations, to ticket counters, to entrances of buses and rail cars. By 2010, Amtrak will be required to have all of its rail cars accessible to people with disabilities, including lavatories and dining cars. Likewise, it is not only the airports of the future that will require design modifications to assist passengers with disabilities; the aircraft interior itself presents a unique platform for unprecedented design challenges to accommodate an aging and ever more mobile population.

Ultimately, the challenge for design professionals is to create environments for people with disabilities that provide for easy, efficient access that flows seamlessly, and which, most important, contributes to a sense of independence and dignity.

### Peter A van der Meulen
*Human Factors Engineer, Tecmath of North America, Inc, Troy, Michigan*

Owing to an increasing amount of global business travel and a growing number of wealthy middle-aged people and pensioners, flying is becoming a common means of travel for a large part of the population, not just a luxury for the happy few.

Consumers used to be forced to adjust to a product or environment (squeeze into a car, watch whatever was on TV); now they can adapt products or environments to suit their individual preferences (adjust a car seat, buy a customized PC). Increased flexibility of manufacturing systems and information technology enable the creation of customized products, using mass-production and mass-assembly methods. Our environment is increasingly comfortable and adjustable to individual needs, and the future consumer, who is also the future airline passenger, expects the same level of comfort and adjustability in airports and aircraft as in other environments. Car manufacturers, clothing companies, shoe and furniture manufacturers are meeting the demand for increased comfort and adjustability by offering customized products. Car seats have memories for different positions, clothes and shoes can be customized to a person's body size, and PCs can be ordered based on customer specifications.

Designers of airports and aircraft not only have to pay special attention to elderly and disabled passengers; in a future of customized products and environments, every single person is a special case, with individual needs and preferences that need to be accommodated. Airports and airlines will have to think about 'customized accessibility'. Check-in stations for the elderly, information in multiple languages, waiting areas with different ambiences, more meal and movie selections on board, and different seats and/or seat pitch to accommodate passengers with a variety of body sizes – all of these will contribute to the passengers' sense of being able to adjust the flight experience to suit individual preferences.

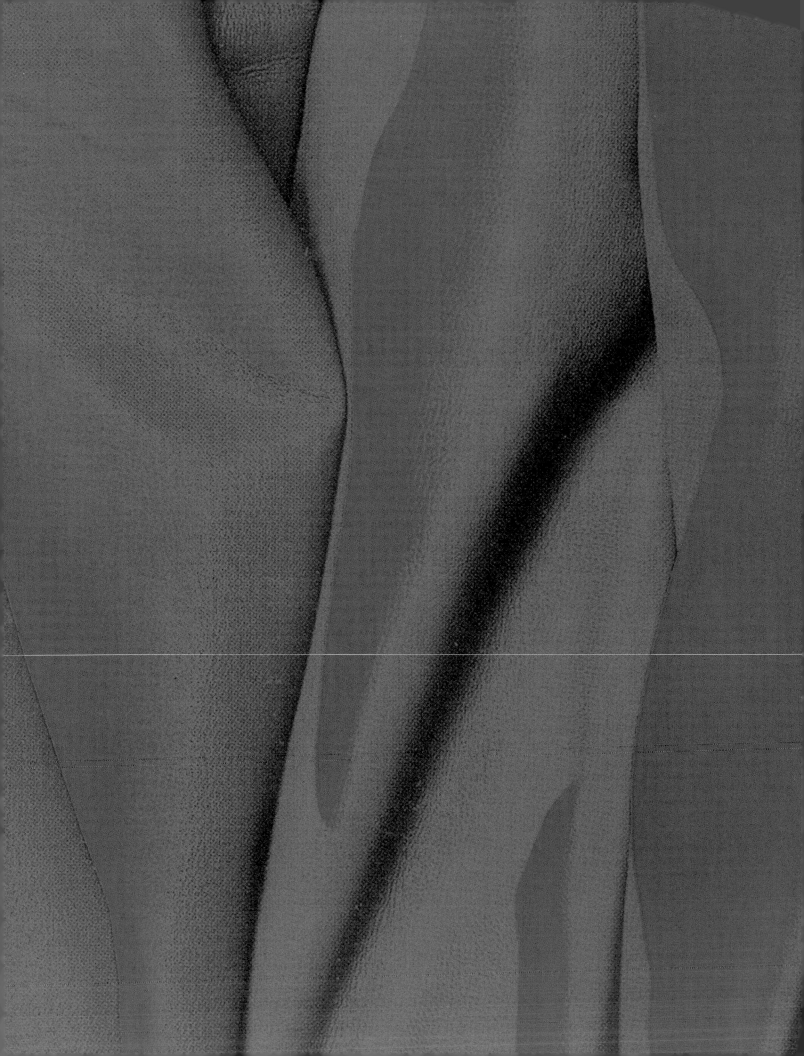

# Cabin Maintenance

Courtesy United

# Chapter 9
## LOOK SMART
### Keep Clean

*When preparing a Boeing B747 for departure, an airline might board more than 25,000 individual items, from in-flight literature, headrest covers, blankets and toiletries to food-and-beverage supplies and the very last toothpick. With a full passenger load on a long-haul flight, the aircraft interior can rapidly become untidy. Flight attendants are accustomed to clearing up at all hours. A dirty cabin, however, is not just unsightly; it presents major problems on many levels.*

Walking into a sparkling-clean aircraft is an exhilarating experience. Customers immediately feel reassured that this is an airline that knows how to take care of its fleet. By contrast, when the cabin is greasy or dusty, customers are bound to wonder whether a similar level of neglect might affect the aircraft's engines or instruments. Keeping a cabin clean is not a matter of one huge initiative but of infinite attention to detail, both in design and in execution. Everyone admires a clean machine, and over the years some airlines have developed a tremendous reputation for excellent cabin cleaning standards. Among the international leaders are Japan Airlines, Lufthansa, SAS and Singapore Airlines.

These days, all airlines can aspire to improved standards. There are many high-tech cleaning products on the market, and many of the aircraft currently flying have never had smoking passengers on board, and as a result all the surfaces of the cabin are much cleaner than they used to be. In particular, the interior of the ducting systems and the lenses of light fittings do not have that grimy patina and yellowish fuzz that used to build up in the aircraft

of previous decades. (Could this perhaps be one of the reasons for the popularity of the yellow, orange and brown decor schemes that were flown by so many airlines during the 1970s?) On the minus side, however, passenger loads are now much greater, turnaround times have been drastically reduced and cleaning crews are frequently disaffected. For personal protection when they travel, some passengers carry clean scarves or handkerchiefs to spread over the tops of their seat backs – a modern-day equivalent of the original antimacassars.

### NEW STANDARDS

Following the progress made by the no-smoking lobby during the 1990s, consumer groups are now calling for independent verification of hygiene standards. To deal with these growing demands, airlines need to demonstrate, at all levels of the organization, their unequivocal commitment to rigorous, ongoing fleet cleaning standards. To deal with the requirement for aircraft to *be* clean, and to *look*, *feel* and *smell* clean, station-cleaning programmes have to be

Courtesy United

linked directly to the airline's ongoing maintenance/change-out and deep-cleaning programmes. There is a need for a clear definition of standards for all departments concerned.

### Change-outs

If an airline changes 30 per cent of its seat covers every 30 days, and if all headrest and pillow covers are changed at the end of every working day on short-haul services, or after every sector on long-haul services, the cabin-appearance manager (or equivalent officer) can structure the cleaning contracts at line stations to tackle normal, and critical-incident, problems of the day. However, in practice, at many carriers the change-out intervals are likely to be less rigorous than those stated above.

### Rapid reporting

Airlines aiming for excellence need to constantly upgrade their reporting systems. In this way they will ensure that corrective action can be taken, on a real-time basis, for high-impact, passenger-visible areas such as door panels and door liners, curtains and cabin dividers. For truly urgent items, a message from the flight deck to the destination station can make all the difference between having a replacement carpet footprint waiting at the entrance to the jetway bridge, and flying the next sector with bad soiling in the cross-aisle.

### Cleaning logs

Air Canada prides itself on its cleaning standards, and has a special department dedicated to the task of cabin maintenance. Ford Chown, President of Linford Aerospace Consulting Services, Inc, and retired Chief Engineer, Interiors, for Air Canada, describes one of the airline's key tools: 'There is a cabin log book in which flight attendants record snags in the cabin, including soiled areas and unserviceable items. The comments are then incorporated into the next cleaning checklist. In this way, the airline can focus on customer concerns in the cabin.'

At airlines where there is no established mechanism for communicating cleaning problems, employees can become very dispirited. When the information does somehow manage to flow through the system, a prompt acknowledgment is a way of rewarding crew members for their vigilance. Cleaning audits need to be undertaken meticulously, and there is no real substitute for line managers 'walking the job' when cleaning crews are working on board the aircraft. The work has to be linked directly to the amount of time that the aircraft is scheduled to spend on the ground. In these days of reduced turnaround times, cabin cleaning has to be carried out with the kind of dedication and high-speed skill demonstrated by mechanics who service the pit stops at Grand Prix car-racing events.

### Deep cleaning

For deep cleaning, and to deal with the chronic issues of natural deterioration and the normal time-scales for wear and tear, there is a requirement for a separate work programme that is linked to the airline's standards of durability.

### Really horrible problems

Examples of more serious problems include stains that originate from leaking lavatories; grunge from air-conditioning systems dripping through the overhead panels; insect infestation in the galley stowage spaces – a problem that can dog aircraft units serving hot, humid stations where the catering load includes fresh fruit and vegetables; flooding toilets and foul odours; and blocked galley sinks. For individual aircraft units where there is a history of trouble, a forward tracking system will ensure that all employees who are in the loop are also ready to deal immediately with the specific problem when the culprit aircraft arrives at their station.

### JETLINER DESIGNERS TO THE RESCUE

Designers can do a lot to make, or break, the appearance standards of an airline. In today's tough commercial environment, airline managements should insist on specifying 'cleanability' as one of the leading headings for any design platform. For example, all lines and surface contours should be smooth and flowing, and therefore easy to clean; there should be a minimum number of indentations, ridges and pockets where dirt and debris can collect. It should be remembered, however, that on smooth surfaces it can be hard to hide and repair the damage from scratches and gouges. Designers should be encouraged to develop camouflage treatments for areas that are likely to suffer from high levels of soilage and abuse.

This approach does not mean that the airline can skip its cleaning routines. But, on a temporary basis, the following techniques will help to keep the cabin looking clean.

### Hard plastics

These are used for tray-tables, seat side panels, armrest covers, bump strips (surface mounted protective coverings), kick strips and head-level bin strips (which run along the edge of baggage stowage bins). Mid-range or darker colours will have a longer life than pale shades. Speckled surfaces are also very practical.

### Curtains

It makes good sense to avoid having light colours where people's hands actually touch the fabric. The fastening systems need to be strong enough to withstand constant usage. As Ford Chown points out: 'Loose-hanging drapes are a real eyesore and spoil the cabin appearance faster than any dirty smudge!'

Shown here are some practical choices for surface treatments inside jetliner cabins: wood-look finish on bin strips running along the edge of the overhead baggage stowage bins; speckled surfaces on tray-tables; a horizontal metal capture strip to secure the join where two wall coverings meet and to prevent fabric from fraying at the edges; sturdy hanging rails and hooks for curtain installations

Courtesy Air Canada/Lantal Textiles

*In business-class cabins, passengers often put their feet on the panels which extend from under the seat. For this reason it is important to select a practical seat-cover fabric which will not look unsightly before the end of the flight or the working day of the aircraft. This resilient fabric used by Air Canada is both handsome and durable; it displays a blended range of forest-green shades which relate to the airline's corporate branding programme (see also the airline's tail fin as displayed at the beginning of Chapter 4/Aero Identity)*

### Seat-cover fabrics, carpets and decorative surfaces

In addition to selecting practical colours, it helps to consider using surface patterns that are 'forgiving'. Liquid stains do not arrange themselves in squares, stripes and geometric layouts. Organic or 'fertile' shapes, such as leaves, marbled patterns, blended streaks and swirls, are less likely to show the outlines of spilled beverages, handprints, chewing gum and other problems.

### Cabin dividers

These partitions, sometimes called cabin walls, bulkheads or vertical surfaces, offer many options for decorative treatments. However, there is a world of difference between the rear-facing front walls and the front-facing rear walls:

- front walls – shoe marks on the laminates that cover rear-facing vertical surfaces can be a perennial problem. Many airlines install a specially certified rug-, gros-point- or tapestry-type fabric up to approximately ankle level. In effect, this is a kind of upholstered kick strip. The fabric is normally in a practical colour that is easy to brush down. In recent years this special covering has been extended upward to reach knee level, and is frequently secured by a metal capture strip that reduces the potential for fraying or torn edges. Nowadays some airlines even use these fabrics from the floor level to the top of the cabin dividers;

- back walls – because the front-facing vertical surface of the cabin divider is usually safely positioned behind the last row of seats in the cabin, it is unlikely to suffer from shoe marks, although there may well be handprints from passengers grabbing at a support structure as they make their way along the aisle. These surfaces can provide an excellent opportunity to display decorative markings or airline insignia, or to install magazine racks and even pegs for coat hangers. They do not need the same utilitarian treatments that have to be used for the rear-facing vertical surfaces.

*This special aviation-grade gros-point-type fabric can be used to cover dado panels and cabin dividers. During the cleaning cycle, it can be brushed down or vacuumed*

*This rear-facing decorative bulkhead wall (with inset closet doors) is covered with a practical granite-like ('Tedlar'-type) plastic film. The horizontal line of small blocks running between the TV sets adds an element of precision to the overall presentation. Some transport specialists believe that a decorative artificial horizon line clearly positioned at the front of the cabin can help air travellers avoid feelings of motion discomfort*

Courtesy United

**Overhead bins**

Aircraft arrive from the manufacturer with bin linings of pristine white, cream or pale grey. However, as soon as passengers start to put their cabin baggage into the overhead compartments, the scuffs, gouges and discolouration spoil the effects of all normal cleaning programmes. Passengers always look inside the bins. It is difficult, and extremely expensive, to change bin interiors, therefore it would help if darker colours could be specified from the outset.

**Placards and signage**

When pressure-adhesive placards are dog-eared and scruffy, the aircraft will never look tidy. Over the years, successive generations of placards make their way into the cabin of every aircraft, and it is not unusual to see sticky marks where old placards have been removed. When several different typefaces and/or colour schemes are displayed in close juxtaposition, the effect can be confusing. Most airlines ensure that signs giving mandatory instructions, such as 'Fasten Seat Belt for Takeoff and Landing' and 'No Smoking', are kept in top condition. However, informational and discretionary signs, such as 'Magazine Rack', 'Coat Closet', 'Timetables' and instructions inside the lavatories also need to be kept in good shape.

At the time of introducing new placards, it can help to make them one size larger than the old templates to conceal the outline left from the previous application. Rounded corners are usually preferable to the classic, 90-degree shape as the labels are less likely to peel off, and the arc shape provides less of a temptation to passengers who try to pick at things on walls and doors. Tremendous internal discipline is required to run placard programmes in an efficient way.

According to Ford Chown: 'Mandatory placards are a requirement of the airworthiness regulations and are therefore required for certification. They are intended to be a focal point for passengers' awareness of something. Marketing people who are concerned with decor sometimes think that placards spoil the effect of their work because they divert the customers' attention away from some of the aesthetic elements in the cabin. Because of the growth of international travel, passengers are likely to feel that there is an increased need to display multi-language placards. Designing effective placards and signs can become difficult when an airline needs more than one language. The use of pictograms is a good way to deal with this issue.'

Courtesy Schneller, Inc.

*Well-maintained placards and stick-on labels can help make a cabin look efficient and passenger-friendly (see pictures above and on the opposite page lower left and right). A scuffed surface on an aisle food cart (above) does not help an airline's image. The hard floor covering (above far right) looks 'trendy' but in fact plays an extremely important safety role on board the aircraft (as explained in this Chapter)*

### Galleys

Using a dark colour for the laminates or surface coverings up to counter level can help to preserve the look of these heavy-use areas. Paler colours can be used from the counter up to ceiling level.

### Aisle carts

These are a problem for even the most sophisticated of carriers, because of the industrial-type handling and hosing that take place in flight kitchens. Sticky labels can become a real mess. Metal 'slot-in' label holders are useful here, but the carts will always need regular and frequent deep cleaning, as well as refurbishment of the side panels.

### Entryways, passageways and aisle carpets

Using removable doormats and drugget or cover strips during turnaround time will help to prevent the tracking of grease and soil. Small carpet footprints can be changed out more easily than large ones. Efficient serging of the edges, together with stain-resistance treatments, will help to maintain appearance standards.

### Non-carpet floor covering

Textured hard floor coverings provide an anti-skid surface, which is essential for the safety of the cabin crew. Used for the galley and lavatory areas, the hard floor coverings usually have raised 'moon dots', basket-weave ridged surfaces or 'grainy granules'. All of these surfaces need careful and regular scrubbing.

### Metal touchpoints

For seat-belt buckles, handles on window shades, safety grab bars and knobs and shelves in lavatories, a semi-matte, brushed-aluminium-type finish will show fingerprints and marks less readily than a shiny, chrome-type finish.

### Lavatory surfaces

Marble- and granite-look surface treatments are better than metal-finish surfaces when it comes to hiding splash marks and stains from toiletries and cosmetics.

### Cabin-friendly scents

Perfumes for toiletries such as liquid soap and skin lotion need to be carefully selected. Some of the commercially available products

Courtesy United

*The colours and textures of the seat-cover fabrics shown in these pictures are not just elegant and distinctive; they are supremely practical in that during long flights they will help camouflage staining and fingermarks*

Courtesy Qantas

give off aromas that are too powerful for an enclosed environment such as an aircraft cabin, considering that a portion of the air is constantly being recirculated.

### Headrest covers

Bright colours, such as red, blue, yellow and green, with small-scale patterns, will look cleaner for longer than pale, solid colours such as white, cream, pink and grey.

### Multi-pockets in seat backs

To the airlines, these are 'in-flight literature pockets'. In particular, this is the place where the flight-safety card is positioned – a regulatory requirement. If the safety cards are not correctly positioned, the aircraft is not permitted to fly. But to the passengers the seat-back pockets are one of the few elements in their temporary, miniature flying universe over which they can exercise total, personal control throughout the flight. Obviously passengers need special stowage spots for all the little personal things that they carry with them while travelling: spectacles, newspapers, books, sandwiches, slippers, sweaters, cameras, medication, cassettes, CDs, laptop computers and so on. Therefore the cabin is a much tidier place when airlines offer several pocket options.

At one time, bungee-elastic web seat-back literature pockets appeared in all classes of service. It was easy for everyone to see just what was inside – no nasty surprises. This approach was particularly popular with cleaning crews because all the dust, dirt and debris simply fell through the gaps in the fishnet receptacle, and though this meant that carpets required regular vacuuming, this was nevertheless preferable to digging inside seat pockets that were closed in and made of solid material.

Although bungee elastic is practical, it was not considered elegant. During the 1980s and 1990s there was a demand for greater product differentiation, and seat pockets became progressively more refined. The structure of the pocket was sometimes incorporated into the overall cutting-and-sewing process of the seat covers. Different styles were certified to fly, some with pleats, gussets and 'knicker-elastic tops'. And there was also the famous 'Iron Lady' – a seat pocket with a horizontal metal spring rod across the top, which, when handled at the wrong angle, could trap the fingers or break the fingernails of unwary passengers.

Invariably, passengers fill all the pockets they can find. Some parents even try to fit their babies into the 'kangaroo pouches'! Interestingly, bungee-elastic web seat pockets are, once again, very à la mode in all classes of service, due to the great emphasis on flying slimline seats. After all, airlines can gain an inch or two of perceived seat pitch, knee room and leg room by not having bulgy, sagging, 'solid' seat-back pockets hitting passengers on the shins every time they try to move.

*BELOW LEFT: Brightly coloured headrest covers provide a lively contrast within a cabin that has been given monochromatic seat-cover treatments (see also Chapter 3/Economy-Class Value)*
*BELOW RIGHT: Passengers normally use all the stowage space they can get their hands on: several small seat-back pockets can help keep personal possessions well organized*

Courtesy Continental

This bungee-elastic web seat-back pocket installed at floor level is large enough to accommodate a regular-size briefcase. BELOW: Other styles of literature pockets come in many shapes and sizes. Motion-sickness bags, which are positioned in these pockets, can be used by passengers when they wish to dispose of chewing-gum, used tissues and sticky wrappers

## A CLEANER TOMORROW

The passenger cabin is a brutally tough working environment. The problems are never-ending, creating a necessity for all the new, high-tech materials, products and cleaning appliances that are now coming onto the market. In future years, with bigger aircraft and longer stage-lengths, we might well see a move toward on-board cleaning personnel, plus the development of hospital-type filters and lighting systems that can kill bacteria and germs.

## COMMENTS FROM THE SPECIALISTS

### Susan Henry

*Managing Director, Onboard Services and Catering, Northwest Airlines*

At Northwest, the focus for the future will be to work with manufacturers on developing materials and cleaning procedures that are easier to maintain and less labour-intensive. We believe that product improvement can come from close collaboration with our suppliers. Ideally we would have carpets that ate dirt and windows that cleaned themselves. The need to keep aircraft in high-utilization profiles reduces opportunities for deep cleaning, and much responsibility for appearance rests with the line stations that are under multiple time constraints to transit aircraft.

### John Varley

*General Manager UK, Meridiana SpA*

Maintaining high cleaning standards can be a constant and pressured situation for a very active downline station. At Meridiana, the aircraft do not start their working day at London Gatwick, and the station cleaners there are required to turn the aircraft around with 45 minutes of scheduled landing time. Given the constant challenges of the European air-traffic-control systems, this turnaround time is frequently reduced to about 20 minutes.

Our policy is to serve somewhat elaborate meals, and with many stage lengths over the Alps at only 26,000 feet (7,925 metres), spillage and stains are a frequent occurrence. Great attention has to be paid to restoring dirty seats to a serviceable status at every turnaround. The Gatwick station does not stock spares and, even if it did, the cleaners would not have the time to change a seat cover under normal circumstances. Cleaning time inside the cabin has been further reduced by new security procedures, which require actual inspection of the seat pockets and other passenger storage areas on each turnaround. Most difficult to handle are heavy spills and stains: the solution at times is to cover the area with a towel or pillow in order to make the seat available for the next flight out.

### David Deignan

*Vice President, Operations, North America, South African Airways*

From an operations standpoint, the airline wants a cabin with a quality interior – one that is easy to maintain and will continue to look new. I think that the marble and granite finishes in bathrooms are superior to the old metal. Darker colours hide imperfections and help to ease the maintenance burden across the fleet. When designing patterns for fabrics it is possible to achieve a pleasing aesthetic effect that at the same time will work successfully on a practical level. The finished products should look good in the cabin environment but should also perform to the technical standards as defined by the airline, for example the number of laundry or dry-cleaning cycles that are scheduled per year.

An airline's head office should ensure that outstations are informed about how best to maintain the cabin interior. For example, in the case of leather, do you treat the synthetic product the same way you would treat the real thing? Our Millennium Product has touches of leather in the first- and business-class cabins. The 'local' cabin cleaners need to know how to keep these surfaces looking new. I remember flying Air New Zealand in the 1970s, and they had sheepskin covers on first-class seats – very comfortable, natural and luxurious, and always kept in immaculate condition.

In addition to ground-service and maintenance teams, cabin crews on long-haul flights need to be proactive in keeping the cabin clean and tidy. Passengers held prisoner in their seats on full long-haul flights have little opportunity to discard the detritus from their meal trays, old newspapers and magazines, and usually put these items in the seat-back pocket or on the floor! The crew should pass through the cabin often to collect these used items, keeping the cabin looking smart and clean.

Courtesy SAS

*This hi-tech self-service buffet bar represents a new era of product development. Bars, like galleys and lavatories, have to be designed to meet and exceed defined standards of cleanliness, practicability and safety certification requirements. The provision of a self-service option throughout the flight is a boon to passengers, and it is considered socially acceptable to congregate in this spot. Airline finance specialists, however, are faced with difficult decisions: how to handle the age-old trade-off between convenience to passengers versus revenue for the company. Would it be more profitable to use the space for more seats? (Market research findings, however, indicate that passengers tend NOT to side with airline finance specialists in matters of this nature!)*

# Chapter 10
## DURABILITY

*Standards of durability are only now starting to be fully analyzed in the context of the passenger cabin. What are the implications for vendors and suppliers? How do airlines stand to benefit?*

The subject of *durability* attracts a great deal of attention when things go wrong. Areas such as affordability, accountability, certifiability, dimensional stability, accessibility, serviceability, cleanability, maintainability, repairability, replaceability and so on can be assessed and quantified fairly accurately for budget purposes. Durability, however, tends to languish in a kind of twilight zone, which can make this part of the budgeting process extremely difficult.

In their drive to achieve weight savings (in order to improve flight performance), airlines have, over the years, moved away from installing heavy, old-style carpets, curtains and seat covers in the aircraft interior. Some of the new-style, lightweight materials tend to be less robust than their predecessors, so questions relating to durability need to be viewed in the context of current reality and customer expectations.

How often do manufacturers and suppliers specify standards or test details relating to durability? When new products are introduced into service, the general expectation is that airlines will deal with durability requirements through experience (the 'school of hard knocks'). And in the absence of accepted industry standards, suppliers still tend to field questions and accusations on a case-by-case basis. However, later on, when products have become

standard features of a cabin interior programme, it should be possible for the client airline and the supplier to jointly establish durability benchmarks and define guarantees or, at the very least, scope out some realistic expectations.

### AN AGENDA FOR DURABILITY

Suppliers can take a competitive stance at both basic and sophisticated levels. Jack Raia, Director, Modification Engineering and DAS Administrator at Timco Engineered Systems, Inc, advises that 'As early as the first article inspection, all details such as the finishing of edges, the use of capture strips, and the treatment of corners and end-cap moldings should be clearly agreed with the designers. The airline will then avoid the problem of flying with unsightly fraying threads hanging out at the edges of fabric or carpet coverings on surfaces such as cabin dividers. Floor coverings need similarly detailed care. Where possible, a modular approach should be used for the design of items that are in the "high wear/usage" category. In this way, refurbishment and replacement can be handled in a timely manner at shorter maintenance services. For example, decorative bulkhead coverings can be organized in removable pieces to facilitate replacement of the areas where

Courtesy SAS

handprints become an eyesore or when there is a need to display a new identity; and seat covers can be constructed in sections so that the soiled areas can be removed, according to need.'

At the mega-carriers, which fly thousands of seats every day, there is a pressing need for high reliability and easy maintainability in order to significantly reduce aircraft maintenance costs. These days, airlines cannot afford to roster ground crews for hours on end simply to dress an aircraft interior. Jon Rose, Managing Director at MGR Foamtex Ltd, describes some of the products now available to help address these issues: 'For quick-change dress-cover systems, our TUS2000, with quarter-turn fasteners, can offer great benefits to operators. Our Style Cover system is available in both two-dimensional and three-dimensional forms. The covers are separated into positive covers, those that directly interface with the passenger, and negative covers, those that surround the rear and the side of the seat. Using this system, it is possible to quickly remove and clean only those parts of the cover that are actually dirty. This approach will help to significantly reduce dry-cleaning costs and increase the overall life expectancy of the seat covers.

'And PEGS (Positive Ergonomic Guide System) features a series of molded plastic pegs fixed to the underside of the bottom cushion. Each configuration of pegs and receptacles has its own unique colour code; the installation times are dramatically reduced compared with the time taken to change Velcro-retained cushions, and the cushion foams will be correctly located from a certification perspective, such as at over-wing exits.'

According to Ryan Ferrara, Manager, New Business Development, at Schneller, Inc: 'Durability is the best example of a property that airline maintenance personnel are most concerned with – but it is the least defined. For laminates and plastics, there are tests for abrasion, scratch and impact resistance. However, within each category there is ambiguousness in identifying accepted test methods.'

Ryan Ferrara points out that in this area aviation lags behind other forms of transportation, for example passenger rail: 'In France, the SNCF and RATP have adopted NF F31-112 test procedures and methods of assessment for material reactions to graffiti-removal products. Products are evaluated and given a rating based on spectrophotometer readings, not subjective interpretation.' Airlines face additional complications that stem from having to meet strict flammability, smoke and toxicity requirements. Ryan Ferrara believes that there is a general need to move toward industry standards: 'In order to predict their future budget requirements, airlines want to be able to measure both cleanability and durability. More and more often, suppliers are being asked to demonstrate, and substantiate, why their particular products should be used. For example, our new graffiti-removal programme is targeted to do the job with only two wipes. Our mission is not only to meet but to exceed the standards required by our clients.'

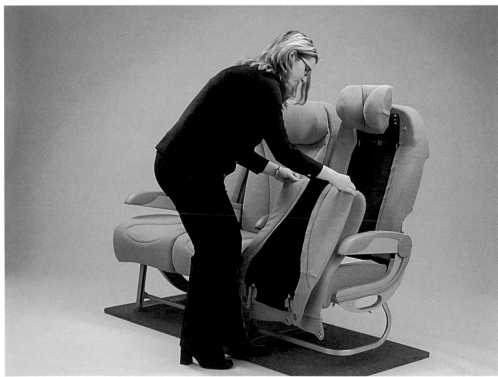

Courtesy MGR Foamtex

Courtesy MGR Foamtex

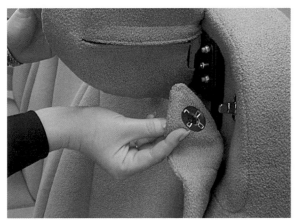

Courtesy MGR Foamtex

*In an effort to reduce aircraft maintenance costs, airlines constantly try to implement faster change-out systems for on-board items such as seat covers and headrest covers (some of the new techniques are described in this Chapter)*

## NEW TEXTILE TECHNOLOGY

Not surprisingly, durability and wearability have always been among the main selling points associated with the development of synthetic fabrics. During the years when airlines were reluctant to depart from their traditional, natural fabrics, there was a need for solid data on abrasion, snagging, fuzzing, pilling and so forth in order to convince purchasing departments that the new high-tech products would successfully survive the rigours of air travel.

Patrice La Susa, Director, Commercial Aviation, at Tapis Corporation, describes how under test conditions, UltraSuede, one of a number of synthetic products currently on the market, is now achieving 200,000 'double rubs' (rubbing in one direction and then back again, allowing an assessment relating to the entire life-cycle of a product): 'Although the fabric looks luxurious, it is extremely hard-wearing, in some cases flying for up to four years without having to be replaced,' she explains. 'One of the reasons for the high performance level is that the micro-fibre structure is inherently stain-resistant. Even red wine does not get absorbed. Stains can be treated on board the aircraft: use a mixture of soap and water, with a clean cloth. Blot first, rub gently, then use a brush to bring up the pile.

'UltraSuede was developed as a result of designers and airlines wanting to create a luxurious look and comfortable feel for first-class seat accents and furniture trim. And our UltraSuede BHC [suitable for bulkhead application] was developed in response to the requirement to have soft, suede-like surfaces in areas of the cabin that need to meet the most stringent aviation flammability requirements. Many traditional fabrics, including leather, cannot consistently meet these requirements, so designers used to specify hard surfaces. Working with our mill specializing in high-tech micro-fibre products, Tapis was able to manufacture a new version of the standard UltraSuede. Our UltraSuede BHC, coupled with advanced flame-retardant technology, emerged as the first soft furnishing to comply with the difficult flammability requirements while offering the aesthetic appeal that the airlines and the designers were seeking. This product made its debut on the British Airways pod sleeper seat in 1995, and it can now be seen in the first-class cabins of such airlines as ANA, Emirates, Qantas, Singapore and United.'

### Synthetics

Finding new ways to extend the working life of an installation is an important objective in any durability exercise: one synthetic product, UltraLeather, which is resistant to bleach and disinfectant products, is in some cases now surpassing vinyl as a fabric of choice for baby-changing, massage and ambulance tables. But how does UltraLeather compare with the genuine article? Patrice La Susa provides an analysis: 'UltraLeather can outlive, underweigh, and cost less than genuine leather. An average-grade cowhide prices out between US$3.95 and US$5.95 per square foot (929 square centimetres), while UltraLeather typically runs at US$4.40 per square foot. Factor in the up to one-third waste

Courtesy U-Land/Tapis Corp

Courtesy Continental Express/Tapis Corp

*These pictures show seat covers made of artificial suede (above left) and artificial leather (above right). Recently developed fabrics of this type are now approved and certified to fly in jetliner cabins (as described in this Chapter)*

experienced in leather use, and your price for leather is increased by a third, or US$1.20 to US$2, depending upon quality. Add your weight savings – less than one-half the weight of leather – and UltraLeather is an engineer's and purchasing agent's dream. In addition, you do not have to compromise quality and aesthetics when selecting leather imitation. UltraLeather's soft hand, natural grain and excellent durability make it ideal for seating, trim and bulkhead applications.'

### Hard plastics and decorative treatments

New lightweight surface-imaging techniques are being developed with durability as a key product feature. Surface areas can be made virtually indestructible as a result of technically advanced ink-dipping and burning processes. Electroplating can provide a silver- or gold-like finish, and three-dimensional coating options can provide tactile features such as supple leather or dense rubber. Or a special film-transfer process can make a treated object look like stone, wood, marble, fabric, leather or paper, with or without patterning; for example, in the late 1990s in the mock-up cabins at Airbus, this new-style approach was featured on dado panels and trim moldings, and in entryway areas, to provide an elegant but hard-wearing wood-look finish. At the end of the decade, Swissair introduced this type of treatment into commercial service, presenting a luxurious-looking, burled-wood finish on the exterior shell of its then state-of-the-art first-class sleeper seats. Clearly, there are exciting possibilities for future developments.

*Long associated with marine and rail transport and the dashboards and accessory fittings of expensive automobiles, a wood-look finish can connote a feeling of glamour, solidity and worth. In the aviation world, wood-look products, fittings or parts have to be lightweight and comply with all mandated safety certification standards*

Courtesy Swissair/Computergraphics ACA

*A wood-look treatment can add style and substance to even a humble hand-towel dispenser panel. Note the practical speckled finish on the vanity counter (see also Chapter 9/Look Smart: Keep Clean)*

### CASE STUDY: HANDS ON AND FEET FIRST

Because durability measurements are based on experience (either in the laboratory or under actual flying conditions), logic would suggest that the second mouse should get the cheese, but this is not always the case. At one airline with a mixed fleet, everyone was delighted when a new-style economy-class seat was successfully introduced into service on the short-haul routes. The cutaway/fly-away armrests gave the illusion of 'opening up the cabin'; the look was dynamic and modern. Slim individuals were even able to squeeze underneath the armrest to get at the row of seats.

The new seats were greatly praised and, as portrayed in advertising and sales promotional material, helped significantly to reposition the upgraded brand image of the airline. A year later, as a result of popular demand – in particular from the boardroom – the same seats were installed on the airline's wide-body fleet. However, alarmingly, on the very first refurbished aircraft, the aisle-side armrests started to break up at a completely unacceptable rate, and it soon became apparent that there was a major durability problem.

It turned out that flight attendants often had to stand on the armrests in order to reach the overhead stowage bins. This had never been necessary on the smaller, single-aisle aircraft. Along the corridors of power, the arguments raged: sue the seat manufacturer; raise the cabin-crew height requirements; hire new, or roster existing flight attendants who weighed less; add steps at the base of the seats; punch toe holes in the seat side panels; block in the open parts of the aisle-side seats; stop passengers from bringing more than a briefcase on board; and so on.

Eventually the airline decided that vertical support bars should be installed underneath the cutaway armrests. The dramatic look was, of course, completely compromised. For the intrepid marketing executives, however, there was no turning back on the wonderful product styling that they had created for their eager-to-fly customer universe. After pleading in vain for other solutions, the marketing manager mandated that, henceforth, all publicity photographs of the seats had to feature a casually draped coat, blanket or similar item, which would totally obscure the newly installed but extremely old-fashioned problem-solving vertical support bars.

## PREDICTABILITY

In the post-11 September 2001 operating environment, many air-lines have suffered major losses, for example a steep decline in business-class travel – a result of the slowing economy. This has forced airlines to concentrate on the need for cost reductions, and by necessity this includes cutbacks in cabin interior programmes. Everything possible has to be done to ensure that budgets can be predicted accurately. Durability therefore needs to become more than only semi-predictable in order to make a significant contri-bution to the long-term well-being of passengers, airlines, manu-facturers and suppliers alike.

## COMMENTS FROM THE SPECIALISTS

### John Varley
*General Manager UK, Meridiana SpA*

There are two issues that Meridiana continually deals with as a carrier with an average stage length of about two hours. The airline has a heavy focus on British Aerospace 146s, and the aircraft have a very high utilization and a high number of cycles compared with long-haul carriers. Most aircraft start the day at 7 am and finish at about 10 pm, and ideally they are then back at our maintenance facility in Italy.

The principal durability challenge for local stations is small damage to seat covers and particularly to the seat mechanisms. The 16-hour utilization exposes the entire seat to great daily stress. We have been helped, however, by cloth headrest covers in first class, and paper covers in economy class, which reduce wear, tear and dirt on the seat backs. Additionally, the fact that we are a no-smoking carrier eliminates small burn damage.

Constant assault on durability comes also from carry-on baggage. With no closet space and a short-haul passenger mentality, the over-head bins are highly utilized and often stretched to the limits of their capacity. If boarding staff are not alert, damage to the bins can become a reality. For the most part, these structures are well designed for their function. Passenger pressure, however, can fre-quently stretch that function to the breaking point.

### Marisa Infante
*Director, Marketing and Corporate Relations, Hoover Industries, Miami, Florida*

We have long believed that things made well should be made to last. We have actually taken strides in this direction, providing our clients with guarantees of up to 15 years of service life on the longevity of their coverings, based on the materials that are selected and on our own practices of workmanship. It is critical here to design coverings and articles with the end in mind. It is not good enough to say that a maintenance person tore a cover while removing it from the seat. Was that cover designed to be easily removed, or was it too difficult for anyone to manage?

A key point is to plan dressings as subassemblies by areas of greater use. For example, the tops of seat backs can be subjected to heavy wear and tear from luggage being brought down from overhead bins, and from passengers who grab the backs of the seats in front of them when rising from their own seat positions. We recommend sectioning the coverings into subassemblies that can be removed independently of the balance, reducing the overall replacement cost significantly.

Ultimately, the burden of durability must fall on the workman-ship of the coverings themselves. We have seen too many cases of inappropriately spaced stitches that later unravel, or poorly rein-forced corners that are bound to break under even minor stress, not to mention unfinished seams that allow the fabric to unravel. These cost-cutting measures on the part of inexperienced sewing shops leave a poor impression of the type of work that is actually achievable in cabin soft coverings. In many ways, the bar has been placed too low, and it is high time to raise it.

### David Weiner
*Architect, New York*

For the design professional, the subject of durability with respect to material choices poses a unique challenge in the air-craft cabin interior. Unlike conventional structures in which materials can be evaluated in terms of strength and resistance to wear without concern for weight, the aircraft cabin becomes relegated to material choices that must achieve high levels of weight-saving, safety, maintainability and efficiency that few other industries have to match.

The good news is that advances in material manufacturing are making choices for the designer easier and more interesting. New plastic laminates not only feature an infinite number of patterns and colours but offer great weight-savings, fire-resistance and long lifespans as well. Carbon-fibre and graphite technologies have also made tremendous advances, offering both high strength and weight savings. Computer-molded plastic provides easy modular assembly and the potential for exciting new interior shapes and forms. Glass technology is also making advances aes-thetically, particularly in the area of lightweight, maintenance-free tiles and surfaces.

An additional advantage that new materials offer the designer is replacement flexibility, both from a maintenance point of view and a style point of view. Given that the lifespan of a typical air-craft is generally longer than current trends in fashion, the designer can now specify newer materials and technologies to periodically update the aircraft cabin interior more easily for both maintenance and style refurbishment.

Courtesy Mexicana

# Chapter 11
## MAGIC CARPET

*When they are up in the air, do passengers really know what is going on under their feet?*

During a flight, passengers spend most of their time sitting in their seats. If they are not actually sleeping, working, eating or enjoying the in-flight entertainment, they usually try to relax, with their eyes half closed or cast downward in the direction of the cabin floor. For this reason, it is important for airlines to choose floor coverings that will not become unsightly during a hard day of flying. In most parts of the world, airlines use medium to medium-dark shades; blues and greys are currently very popular.

Many aircraft carpets are relatively anonymous, and are selected principally to support the leading elements of the decor scheme of the cabin interior. By contrast, the distinctive carpet that flew in the premier-class cabin of Aer Lingus during the late 1990s was particularly memorable: flax-coloured Celtic lettering flowing across an inky background provided a dramatic surround for the Irish-green leather seat covers.

In earlier years, when installing aircraft carpet it used to be difficult to line up the then-fashionable large patterns that repeated at intervals of up to 3 feet (91.44 centimetres). The problem: how to get the pattern to run around the seat-track covers and the 'monuments'. Fortunately, we are now seeing the introduction of new ingenious small-scale surface patterning, not just equidistant geometric dots and dashes but exciting, computer-generated shapes – free moving, random and omnidirectional. These patterns are guaranteed to cut down on wastage, of both yardage and the time spent on cutting, installation and replacement.

Carpet construction can pose knotty problems for airline purchasing departments. David Sandiford, Manager, Aviation Sales, Mohawk Industries, Inc, Aircraft Carpet Division, outlines the complexities of the manufacturing process: 'Most airlines tend to choose woven carpets over tufted carpets, because woven carpet is inherently more durable. Woven aircraft carpets are typically manufactured with either nylon or wool yarn systems, although nylon has become the choice of the US airlines. All commercial aircraft carpeting must be certified to meet the requirements of FAR (Federal Aviation Regulation) 25.853, Appendix F, Part 1 (12-second vertical burn requirements). To meet this requirement, most manufacturers use a flame-retardant compound added to the back coating of nylon-woven aircraft carpets. Flame-retardant compound may be added to both the backing and the fibre for wool-woven aircraft carpet. These treatments are durable and should not affect the carpet's ability to meet the FAA requirements when the carpet is properly cleaned using such recommended methods as hot-water extraction.'

In wealthier times, many airlines flew a wide range of carpets, from more practical loop pile, with a relatively quiet surface pattern, in economy class, to expensive, cut-pile products, displaying

Courtesy Mexicana

Courtesy Eastern Airlines/SER-MAT

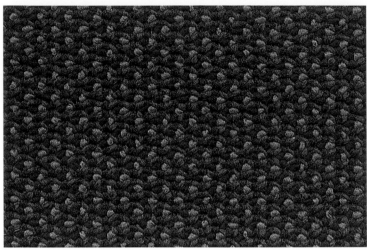

Courtesy Hawaiian Airlines/Mohawk Industries, Inc

*Reincarnated carpets! The carpet on the left was developed and used in the 1970s at Eastern Airlines; a recoloured version (right) is used today at Hawaiian Airlines (this process of carpet reincarnation is explained in this Chapter)*

*RIGHT: Typical cross-section of step with tread-nosing*
*BELOW: For use on aircraft staircase steps: durable polyurethane step-nosing, sometimes referred to as 'bull-nosing' (as explained in this Chapter)*

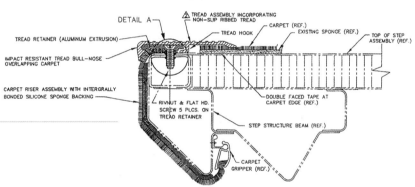

Courtesy Ludlum Products, Inc

Courtesy Ludlum Products, Inc

Courtesy Aer Lingus

glamorous colours and exotic motifs, in the first-class cabin. For business class it was necessary to decide whether to lump this section of the aircraft with economy class (a downmarket approach) or with first class (which was tough on the budget), or add a *third* carpet to the portfolio.

However, due to necessary cost cutting, many airlines now fly one standardized fleet carpet, which runs from the nose to the tail of the aircraft. This pleases the finance department, but the marketing managers and designers have to formulate a plan for using the carpet in all classes of service simultaneously. South African Airways' solution was to fly *two* versions of its splendid all-wool sapphire-blue carpet. In the first-class cabin, the pile depth was significantly greater than in the other parts of the aircraft, connoting a greater sense of luxury for the premium passengers. The non-carpeted hard floor covering in the galley area provided a natural, and inconspicuous, divider strip between the two grades of the single product.

It is even possible to fly parallel products within one zone of the aircraft. For example, at British Airways, in the first-class cabin of the Boeing B747s and the Boeing B777s, the blue wool carpet around the seats is luxuriously textured, a cut-pile product; in the busy aisle areas there is a more resilient version of the product, with a cut-and-loop weave.

Aviation-grade carpeting has to meet all regulatory fire-retardancy requirements. Larry Loschiavo Jr (Larry Lo), Vice President of SER-MAT, a supplier of finished rug parts and bulk carpet for airline cabins, outlines the background to this: 'Initially, through the 1950s, carpet for aircraft was produced on standard looms without any particular requirement for fire-retardancy based on use in an aircraft. The first airline-specific regulations applied only to a horizontal burn test. Today, all fabric on board must conform to FAR 25.853, Paragraph (a), Appendix F, Part 1 (a) (1) (ii).

'The FAR requires candidate material to undergo six individual burn tests – three in the filling direction and three in the warp direction. The test measures how long the material burns, the length of the burn and whether any dripping occurs. The test is done in a special chamber with specification as to the type of flame and composition of the gas and temperature initiating the burn. The fire must self-extinguish within 12 seconds on average for the entire test module.'

When contracts are being negotiated, the price-break levels are, generally, very quantity-sensitive. Depending on construction, weave, backing and provenance, airlines can, in rough terms, expect to pay around US\$25 to US\$30 per square yard or square metre for a carpet that is all wool or a mix of wool and nylon. For an all-nylon product, the cost is likely to be about US\$20 to US\$25.

There are arguments about the virtues of wool versus nylon. Some specialists maintain that for airlines flying high passenger-load factors, nylon carpet can offer excellent wearability and durability standards, especially in heavy-use areas such as the aisles and the

*Colourful carpet patterns can add character and distinctiveness to jetliner cabins (as shown below and in the picture of the PrivatAir aircraft in Chapter 16/Ways Ahead)*

Courtesy Aer Lingus

Courtesy Southwest/Mohawk Industries, Inc.

*For many years Southwest flew this tan-coloured carpet which links directly with the air-craft exterior livery paint scheme of the airline's original corporate branding programme*

turning points. The normal replacement cycle for busy aisles can be approximately 12 to 15 weeks; the use of nylon pile can in many cases extend this to 20 to 25 weeks. Nylon carpet can also provide weight savings, with accompanying savings in fuel burn.

## FOOTING THE BILL

A high load-factor aircraft might carry up to 10,000 passengers per week. From the point of view of the wear on the carpet, this could total 10,000 embarkations, plus 10,000 disembarkations, plus, possibly, the serving of up to 10,000 meals and 10,000 drinks and duty-free items, plus, maybe 10,000 visits to the lavatory. Imagine! The equivalent of up to 50,000 people, or 100,000 feet, impacting a piece of carpet only 18 inches (45.72 centimetres) wide in just one week!

To keep costs down, in the last decade many airlines have started to use a greater number of smaller pieces of carpet instead of the old-style, larger 'footprints'. These can be changed out more readily, even during a rapid turnaround at the gate. But

small carpet footprints require meticulous finishing in order to prevent passenger safety hazards. Traditionally, serging and other such processes were carried out off the aircraft. However, a new generation of machines small enough to be brought on board the aircraft is now being developed, and progress in this field will greatly improve the standards of ongoing maintenance.

Carpets that are very pale, very dark or uniformly solid in colour show staining far more readily than carpets with variegated or marbled surface patterns. It is estimated that approximately 70 per cent of aircraft carpet is thrown out due to staining, and the remaining 30 per cent because the carpet is actually worn out. By having the carpet stain-proofed prior to installation, the throw-away rate can be reduced significantly.

Use of removable doormats, with non-slip backing and a rubber-type surrounding band – preferably in a colour compatible with the fleet decor scheme – keeps soilage and corrosive liquids at bay, particularly at airports where there is remote parking for aircraft, and passengers are obliged to walk across the tarmac in order to board.

Courtesy Southwest/Mohawk Industries, Inc

*In 2002, the new branding programme at Southwest produced a new blue carpet, which was rapidly nicknamed 'Peanuts' (the story is related in this Chapter)*

## ROLL CALL

At large airlines, which buy carpet by the mile, the purchasing departments might well have a policy of multi-sourcing. However, the engineering and maintenance departments are then faced with the challenge of keeping the carpet rolls, and the individual pieces, from getting muddled during busy days in the hangar. Invariably, there is only limited space on the storage racks and in the rug shops. So it is generally agreed that locking an individual supplier into an individual aircraft type is still one of the most reliable ways of maintaining product integrity.

Carpet installation is a specialized task that usually has to be carried out in the hangar at night, so as not to incur unnecessary downtime for the aircraft. Some carriers, in order to emphasize the spaciousness of their first-class cabins, have changed from the traditional strips of carpet running fore and aft and are now flying wall-to-wall carpeting, using big carpet pieces held together underneath by double-sided tape. SER-MAT's Larry Lo recommends that airlines move away from the traditional tan-coloured

tape and instead use black, which he says is 'far more successful – in this way, you just don't see the join lines'.

Even with the modern methods now available, an aircraft staircase can still present a major challenge, as on the Boeing B747, the wide-bodied Ilyushin Il-86 and the forthcoming Airbus A380 (see Chapter 16/Ways Ahead). Staircase carpet pieces suffer greatly when galley carts or passenger carry-on bags with vicious metal corners are dragged up and down between the decks. 'All traffic to the upper-level passenger seating must be funnelled through the stairwell,' says Kenneth Ludlum, President of Ludlum Products Company, Inc, which manufactures aircraft interior parts, primarily plastics. 'This includes maintenance and passenger-service needs before, during and after flight operations. Maintenance of appearance standards can become an expensive and critical problem, with step-nosing carpeting being the focal point of maximum wear and exposing of soil.' On the subject of so-called 'bull-nosing', Kenneth Ludlum explains: 'Durable polyurethane step nosings incorporating reduced edge

*Aircraft carpets must meet all mandated safety certification standards (as explained in this Chapter). Because of heavy usage, colours and surface patterns need to be ultra-practical (as shown opposite). At the same time, the carpet has to coexist in harmony with the accompanying main elements of the cabin decor scheme – a challenging assignment for jetliner designers!*

radii, replacing carpeted nosings, eliminate this major high-wear problem. Well-defined step-nosing edges represent a greater safety level in comparison with easily camouflaged, rounded, carpeted step edges. Non-slip ribbed nosing tread surfaces are another important safety feature. The nosing tread locks firmly in place, requiring familiarity with the tread design for removal for infrequent replacement. To counteract the functional look the nosing can be custom-coloured to match the cabin decor scheme.'

Some aircraft carpet types have been around for a long time, in one form or another. Over the years, a successful product can be recoloured, rescaled or retextured to achieve a veritable 're-incarnation' on a new carrier. For example, at Yemenia, at the turn of the millennium, the carpet on its wide-body Airbus aircraft was most businesslike: a basket-weave, honeycomb look, in gentle shades of blue and grey. The effect was totally up to date, but clearly derived directly from that wonderfully strong, hard-wearing, all-loop, all-nylon carpet that was pioneered by Eastern, in a brown-and-tan combination, at the end of the 1970s. And the fleet carpet at Hawaiian Airlines can claim a similarly distinguished lineage.

## BORDERLINE ACTIVITIES

David Sandiford of Mohawk Industries' Aircraft Carpet Division reminds us that during the course of their careers, some aircraft carpets are awarded memorable nicknames: 'For example, Southwest traditionally flew a tan-coloured carpet with a surface pattern of small, red, geometrically positioned squares – this linked directly with the colour scheme of the aircraft exterior livery. In 2002, to celebrate its 30th anniversary, the company changed to a blue-based livery scheme and began to fly a handsome new blue carpet. The surface pattern resembles a random scattering of golden-coloured seeds or fragments of nuts crushed underfoot. Immediately, the new creation was given the affectionate nickname "Peanuts".'

Other famous airline floor coverings are known in the business as 'Streaky Bacon', 'Dotty Spots and Spotty Dots', 'Pac-man', 'Cosmic Rays', 'Scatterdust' and, currently flying in the first-class cabin of a very grand airline, 'Swirly Worms'! Who can predict which of these magic carpets might still be on flight duty in the next 20 years?

## COMMENTS FROM THE SPECIALISTS

### David Deignan
*Vice President, Operations, North America, South African Airways*
Prior to delivery, carpets must be treated to make them stain-resistant. During turnarounds, either at base or at outstations, the emphasis is on a thorough vacuuming, and rarely is there time to replace or repair stained sections of carpet. The goal should be to have a carpet that continues to look clean and new before each departure. The airline may have to spend more initially, but it will save later on repair and replacement costs.

### Susan Henry
*Managing Director, Onboard Services and Catering, Northwest Airlines*
Carpet selection for a major airline involves thinking ahead. Most of today's manufacturers can meet wearability standards; the challenge is to find a design solution that can look great after a full cleaning and also look good after several long-haul flight segments. Our experience has shown that close attention to colour and pattern can help in making the pattern work to present a crisply maintained appearance. With proper attention to these characteristics, it is possible to pick carpet designs that can be used throughout a multipurpose aircraft fleet.

### John Varley
*General Manager UK, Meridiana SpA*
The carpet challenge at Meridiana was not typical of a long-haul carrier and even differed from that of many short-haul carriers servicing major cities. Although London Gatwick is a major station with the most modern boarding amenities, we serve many popular destinations where passengers enplane and deplane on the tarmac. The change rate on carpet is only two to three times per year, and we find that fighting dirt and dirty water is a larger issue than it might be for carriers with a different route structure. We opted for a very durable fabric and a blue colour that assisted in making a good showing in a tough environment.

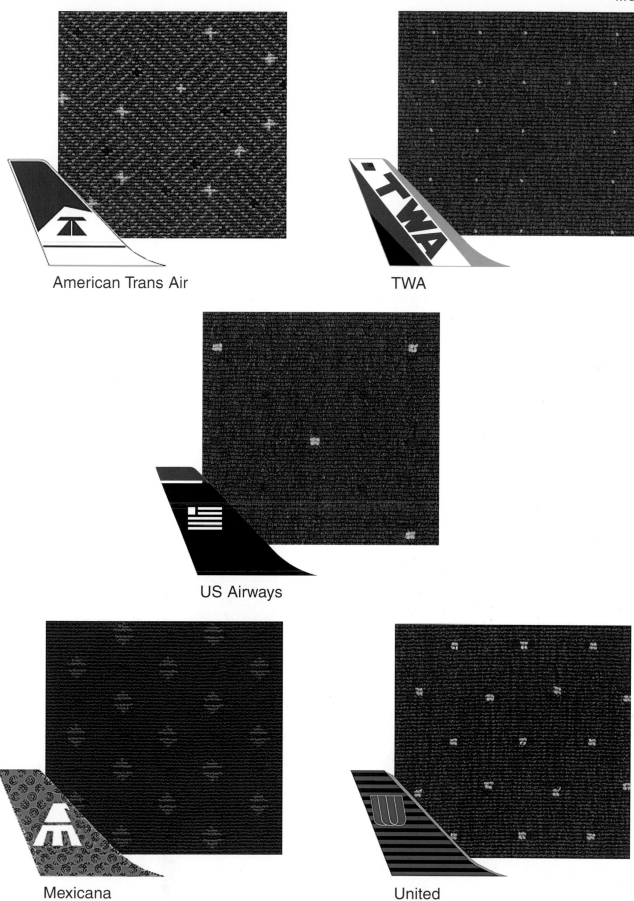

American Trans Air

TWA

US Airways

Mexicana

United

Courtesy Douglass Interior Products, Inc

*Record-setting intrepid aviation pioneers: Charles Lindbergh's non-stop solo flight from New York to Paris on 20-21 May 1927 was a historic landmark; nine years later Beryl Markham flew non-stop solo on the westward track from England to Nova Scotia*

Courtesy Minnesota Historical Society

Courtesy Lenare Studio

# Chapter 12
## THE LEATHER FORECAST

*After being associated almost exclusively with top-level premium travel at the beginning of the 1980s, leather has become a standard feature in business-class cabins. What are the attractions? And will economy class be able to resist?*

Early aviators treasured their leather helmets, gauntlets and flying jackets, which were frequently lined with silk, wool or sheepskin. Open-cockpit flying was a very chilly affair, made possible only by the use of the most efficient forms of insulation available at the time. Even now, in the new millennium, we continue to favour these basic natural materials for use on board aircraft, not just because of the marvellous level of personal comfort they offer but because they can satisfy the most stringent burn-test requirements.

In general aviation, it is usual to see all-leather cabin interiors, often in luxurious pale colours reminiscent of classy sports cars and yachts; because the quantity-measurement requirements for small, privately owned aircraft are minimal, it is easy to throw away seat covers that are stained or scuffed. For scheduled airlines however, current budget constraints mean that a different approach is required.

According to some suppliers, leather seat covers (both genuine and synthetic) cost two or three times as much as cloth but will last up to five times as long. However, this depends on the wear-and-tear factor, and on the airlines' ability to provide suitable maintenance; if the colour is something like pale pearl or blanched almond, even with the special solvents available today the stains will eventually become impossible to deal with, and throwaway rates will be high. Therefore, to avoid wasting money, time and effort, airlines tend to select more practical dark colours that help to conceal fingerprints and many of the normal stains that build up during a flight, particularly with high-frequency service and heavy passenger loads. Even when high-quality cowhides became scarce and price levels greatly increased following the catastrophic outbreaks of foot-and-mouth disease in Europe at the start of the new millennium, the airlines did not stop buying and flying leather seat covers. The payoff is positive in many ways.

There have been endless debates about whether it is better to offer all-leather seat covers or a combination of leather and cloth. The general consensus seems to be that, for shorter flights – those of, say, under four hours – all-leather is quite acceptable. For longer trips, however, and particularly on overnight flights, passengers seem to prefer the cloth-covered central insert panels, which are thought to 'breathe' better than leather.

In recent years, artificial leather and suede have gained certification status, and complete acceptance, in the aviation business. The great advantage of these fabrics is that they are extremely lightweight, enabling airlines to achieve savings in weight and fuel burn. And because they are sold by the yard, there is less wastage during the cutting-and-sewing process than is the case with real cowhides. Nowadays, these high-tech fabrics are used not only for seat covers but also for literature pockets, curtains, cot covers and baby-changing tables.

### FOREVER LEATHER

Looking back over the past two decades, there has been a slow but irrevocable shift in the use of leather on board aircraft. Initially, on the traditional airlines, it was regarded as something very special, the preserve of the premium passengers. Subsequently it was appropriated for use by the forward-looking business-class carriers, and in recent years leather has successfully moved into all-one-class aircraft.

In the early 1980s, Pan Am introduced a dramatic navy blue leather-and-sheepskin seat-cover combination in the first-class cabin of its Boeing B747 fleet. Even the 'bumper roll' around the central console and the footrest area of the extendable seat were covered with leather. The designer was Philip George. At the same time, the airline relaunched its Clipper Class, an exclusive business-class cabin. The bits of leather that were cut from the extremities of the hides used for the first-class programme were brought into Clipper Class and used in conjunction with a herringbone-tweed fabric. Leather was used for stitched-in headrest covers, seat-back pockets, bulkhead-mounted literature pockets and related miscellaneous items such as curtain tiebacks and amenity-kit holders.

In 1990, when Eastern Airlines pioneered the 'Fly First, Buy Coach' concept, the airline's advertising emphasized luxurious new seats, covered in two-tone grey leather, with punched ventilation holes (Mercedes style) in the centre back panel. It was during this decade that leather began to be used as a key element in the design schemes of many leading airlines, as outlined below.

**The first-class cabin**

- At American Airlines, in both the first-class and business-class cabins, there was a taupe leather-and-sheepskin seat-cover combination. Many regular passengers swore that these were among the most comfortable seats they had ever experienced.
- At ANA, the burgundy-and-grey leather upholstery combination added panache to the work stations of the carrier's business corner, and to the stools at the bar counter.
- British Airways featured a combination of dark blue leather and fabric, complemented by a lighter blue trim in artificial suede, at the time of the introduction of the revolutionary first-class pod sleeper seats.
- Delta flew a distinctive seat-cover scheme in burgundy leather, with matching collateral items such as bag-tags and ticket jackets.
- At Gulf Air, a sophisticated grey leather is used in the first-class cabin. Obviously this approach requires more attention than the darker colour schemes. The use of pale-coloured leather signals the highest level of luxury, one that is generally associated with the interior decor of the most exclusive private jets.
- Singapore Airlines created an elegant and unusual ambience in its first-class cabin using leather and suede finishes in exotic fruitwood colours.
- Swissair implemented a powerful-looking first-class cabin layout, inspired by the Eames chair. In the 1940s and 1950s, Eames chairs had leather-covered cushions, set in a molded plywood frame or shell. The Swissair sleeper seats were covered with a relatively plain, navy blue cloth fabric; at each seat position, however, a matching navy leather was used for such accessories as the armrest covers and the ottoman (a movable footstool). (This seat assembly, complete with its leather-covered accessory items, was subsequently flown by the 'phoenix' successor airline Swiss International Air Lines.)
- At United, when the prestigious first-class suites were introduced, the sleeper-seat compartments were upholstered in a combination of leather and suede in blue and beige, a high-tech treatment that can be cleaned of stains on board the aircraft.

Courtesy Eastern Airlines

Courtesy Singapore Airlines

Courtesy Middle East Airlines/Lantal Textiles

**The business-class cabin**

During the early 1990s, the business-class cabins of most airlines flew cloth seat covers. Later in the decade, however, when some of the major carriers dropped first class and switched to two-class service, they began to use leather in order to create an upmarket look. The overall aim was to provide first-class luxury at a business-class fare. Below is a selection of some of the most memorable schemes:

- Aer Lingus Premier Class – all-leather seat covers in a lyrical shade of Irish green (as shown in Chapter 11/Magic Carpet).
- Alaska Airlines – a classic, practical scheme in dark blue.
- Delta Business Elite – an inky-navy leather-covered seat surround with a toning, fabric-covered central insert panel (as shown in Chapter 2/Business-Class Comfort).
- Middle East Airlines – Grey leather with a unique touch: delicate red piping (as shown above), which can require

some special care when there is danger of scuffing or scratching.

- U-Land – a subtle use of artificial suede (as shown in Chapter 10/Durability).
- US Airways – streamlined executive styling in a shade of grey reminiscent of the Concorde interiors at both Air France and British Airways.
- Virgin Atlantic – the dramatic Scarlet Lady-coloured leather adds real pizazz to the Upper Class cabin, not just on the seat shells but in the bar and beauty salon areas as well (as shown in this Chapter, in Chapter 2/Business-Class Comfort and Chapter 6/Sky Lights). The flight attendants' seats, in grey, display a high-fashion, vertical, 'corrugated' treatment that some people describe as the 'leather bondage look'. This may well turn out to be an index to the styles of the future.

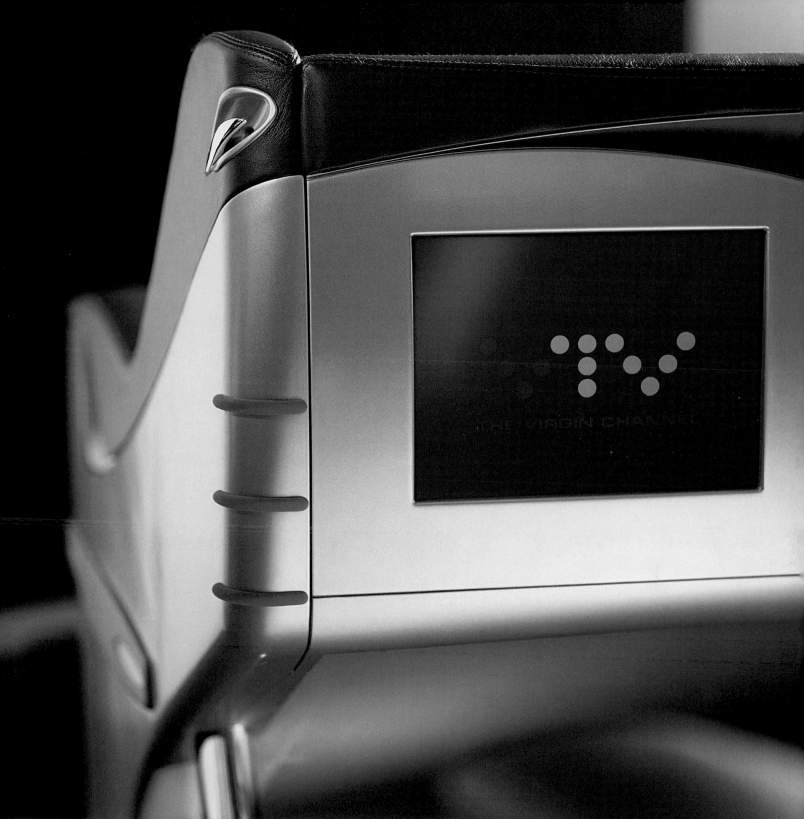

Courtesy Virgin Atlantic

## All-one-class aircraft

In the past few years, leather has made yet another conquest: it is now an undisputed favourite in all-one-class jetliner cabins. At the premium level, the Delta Shuttle, the British Airways Concorde and PrivatAir all fly navy leather seat covers from the nose to the tail of the aircraft. On many of the small aircraft – for example at Adria Airways, Continental Express, Crossair, Mesa Airlines and Tyrolean Airways – leather is used to make the economy-class cabins more closely resemble those of private business jets.

At the beginning of the new millennium, even the *Wall Street Journal* betrayed some measure of excitement when describing the all-leather cabin treatment that was one of the main features of jetBlue, the New York-based, low-cost, low-fare, all-one-class, no-frills carrier that had recently made such a dramatic entry into the industry.

## Beauty treatments

Whether leather is used for seat covers throughout the aircraft or simply for accessories, it is still a long-term investment. If an airline is to get the best return, all maintenance programmes should start on the first day of operation, if not sooner. Monika Luethi, Director of Design, Department of Development, at Lantal Textiles, offers some advice:

*For interim cleaning*: Use a light soapy water, applied with a sponge or a soft cloth. Wipe off the soapy water with fresh water, and dry with a soft cloth.

*For the main cleaning*: Because this is a deep-cleaning process, use the cleaning fluids that are specially recommended for leather. Wet a sponge with the cleaner, and clean the leather with circular movements. *Do not rub!*

Dry gently with a clean cloth. Leave the leather to air-dry for at least 30 minutes. This procedure will help greatly to counteract the effects of the low levels of humidity on board the aircraft.

*Cleaning intervals*: The interval very much depends on the airline's quality standards as well as on the usage of the seats. One airline does interim cleaning every month and main cleaning every six months. Another airline does cleaning every week and main cleaning every three months. In other words, the intervals have to be defined by the customers individually, based on their own standards. As an indication, we suggest doing at least two main cleanings a year.

If the cleaning cycle is neglected, even if stains are relatively difficult to see (as is sometimes the case with dark leather), the look and general suppleness of the material will deteriorate irreversibly.

The use of vacuum nozzle attachments (shaped in rounded plastic, not the kind with sharp metal edges) will clear dust and debris from semi-hidden areas (for example where the seat back meets the seat cushion) and help get rid of crumbs and food particles that make their way into the punched ventilation holes, or into the seam edges and join lines of the upholstery. In particular, regular vacuuming is important when leather is used in conjunction with sheepskin.

Airlines that fly without headrest covers (a practice that is not permitted in many countries but is not uncommon in North America) need to give extra attention to the hygiene standards of the area of the seat back where the passenger's head makes contact with the leather. A good sanitization programme is a must.

## HIDE 'N' CHIC

According to fashion pundits, leather will be with us forever. Improved technology has made this product more affordable, more durable and more fun to work with than ever before. Throughout the world there are signs that the top retail brands have moved on from the Marlon Brando/James Dean biker look and toward modern-style garments aimed particularly at young customers. The old, rigid cowhides have been superseded by a new generation of soft, supple, thin, lightweight, stretchy skins that can be embossed, debossed, distressed, gilded, punched, pleated and textured, in all shades of the rainbow and to suit all tastes.

Today, an advertisement claiming 'All-Leather Interior' automatically confers a cachet of style and sophistication in both the automotive and the airline industries. With regular cleaning, moisturizing and other protective measures – in a way not dissimilar to how we treat our skin – we can ensure that our leather schemes will grow old gracefully, too.

## COMMENTS FROM THE SPECIALISTS

### Steve V Peterson

*Regional Sales Manager, Douglass Interior Products, Inc, Las Vegas, Nevada*

Leather has become almost a standard among airlines in designing new seat applications. Long used for first-class and business-class cabins, it is now being seriously considered for entire aircraft applications. However, the desire of designers and airlines to install this very flexible and popular product is not always matched by an understanding of its characteristics in look and wear.

One of the major misunderstandings about upholstery leather is that it should be completely uniform in appearance. Particularly in the aerospace industry, there can be a tendency to 'over-inspect' some items. Leather will naturally have some variations in the graining, which will have no impact on the strength or wearability of the upholstery. In fact, one of the attractive features of leather used in a cabin is that it gives a warm and comfortable feel to the passengers' perception of the space. Part of this appeal comes from small variations in the look of each seat, which contributes to a less institutional atmosphere in the cabin.

Also, recently there has been a trend toward shaving leather much thinner than is recommended, purportedly for weight savings. Although most tanneries have the physical ability to shave leather very thin, this is not recommended for other than trim applications, such as armrests. Frequently, over-attention to weight savings can lead to overstressed applications that become visible and unsightly. As a result of normal cabin wear and tear, these applications can become high-maintenance replacement items, and can be a strain on the budget.

### Marisa Infante

*Director, Marketing and Corporate Relations, Hoover Industries, Miami, Florida*

We are very much in favour of the trend toward leather interiors, and have helped airlines with such programmes on a massive scale because the material is impressively stain-resistant and can easily be kept clean without the burdens associated with cleaning fabric seat coverings.

For seat sections that are subject to excessive wear and tear, we recommend breaking up the coverings into pieces that can be removed independently of the balance, reducing the overall replacement cost significantly. Materials should be selected to withstand this sort of pressure; leather is excellent at withstanding abuse.

A good seat dress-cover manufacturer should be well versed in the full details of such a process, including being able to converse intelligently with the designer, the structure manufacturer and the airline on whatever questions they may have regarding the suitability for service of the image that is being considered. They should be able to provide balanced recommendations on the use of leather versus other possible materials, based on the airline's preference and the life span envisaged for the image. They should be able to serve the airline as a programme partner, wherever their advice and experience may be of benefit.

Marketing Challenge

Courtesy Braniff/George Design Studio

# Chapter 13
## FLYING COLOURS

*In the new millennium, should airlines continue to use time-honoured colour schemes? Or is there a case for striking out and trying something new? If so, how should the decisions be made?*

In recent decades, great attention has been given to the choice of colours for the interiors of institutional environments. Pink-washed walls in prisons are said to have a calming effect on the inmates, and aquatints are supposed to promote a sense of well-being in spa resorts, hospitals and health centres. Wood-look earth tones are associated with locations that need to be perceived as solid and reliable, for example banks, insurance companies, seats of government and religious meeting places, and silver, gold and platinum trim, as used for designations of rank throughout the ages, and for today's credit cards, proclaim special degrees of prestige.

The first artificial dye colour – derived from coal tar – was discovered and patented in London in 1856. Subsequent mass marketing generated a fortune for its inventor, Sir William Perkin, and 'revolutionized the worlds of fashion, industry and chemical research', as described by Simon Garfield in *Mauve: How One Man Invented a Colour That Changed the World* (2001). Who would then have believed that by 1998 the University of Manchester would launch an electronic dictionary of colours, containing more than 16 million shades?

While there have been extensive studies to explore the effects of the use of colours, textiles and surface treatments in office-type environments – from the standpoint of both employees and consumers – there seem to be no such tracking programmes in the field of aviation. However, the marketing department of Lantal Textiles offers the following guidance:

Understanding the impact of textiles on the overall interior space is increasingly important in both the aviation and the commercial markets. Airlines have to communicate security, safety, brand status and an overall sense of comfort. The cabin interior of an aircraft is confined, and the colour scheme of the multiple rows of seats stands out in the environment. The lighter the colour, the greater the perception of space. Cooler colours with accenting warm ones – within a visually interesting small-scale pattern – are conducive to calming moods and relaxation.

In general, pale colours are associated with luxury, suggesting the need for a retinue of helpers for their upkeep. (Witness the delectable interiors of the top-class charter aircraft, yachts and sports cars in shades of cream, almond and vanilla.) Darker colours are more functional: they help to conceal imperfections and require less maintenance and fewer cleaning cycles, therefore seat covers, rugs and curtains in the busy cabins of the commercial airlines almost always feature deep, strong, serviceable colours.

At the time of launching a new wide-body Airbus fleet, one

Courtesy Braniff/George Design Studio

Courtesy Braniff/George Design Studio

Courtesy Braniff/George Design Studio

Courtesy Braniff/George Design Studio

famous airline installed economy-class seat covers in shell pink. After struggling to clean the daily stains from tea, coffee, milk, orange juice, ketchup, alcohol and chewing gum the airline was forced to write off a substantial amount of inventory. 'We were trying to make it look as roomy as the Boeing B747 fleet,' the marketing boss said plaintively as the engineering department grimly started to rework the part numbers catalogue for a more practical decor scheme that would achieve better standards of maintainability of products and their colours.

Traditionally, US airlines have been among the world leaders in the field of corporate-identity colour treatments. Investor-owned airlines in the US have always faced direct competition, and the use of distinctive colour schemes was one of the quickest ways to carve out an individual identity. For example, in the late 1960s Mary Wells and Harding Lawrence, aided and abetted by a brilliant galaxy of artists and designers including Alexander Calder, Philip George, Alexander Girard and Emilio Pucci, turned the fleet of Braniff International into a dazzling, multicoloured flying work of

art. Other memorable examples include Air Florida, National, Western Pacific and Southwest. Stan Hooper, Interiors Engineering Director at Eastern Airlines, recalls his early work: 'Our DC8 Golden Falcon Fleet featured a specific laminate on every single sidewall panel and ceiling panel, showing mytho-logical scenes and astrological signs. There were gold-coloured window curtains; the seats were covered with gold leather and a gold-blue fabric; there was gold mylar on the overhead bins and light valences; and all the metal trim was anodized! A fantastic kaleidoscope of colours and patterns. Unforgettable!'

By contrast, at government-owned airlines, the general ten-dency is to play it safe. Top appointees from a political or military background usually opt for a relatively bureaucratic or neutral approach. When national chauvinism is on display, the colours of the country's flag or local flora and fauna are frequently presented in a dramatic way on the aircraft exterior. But how often is this approach brought into the cabin interior?

For international airlines, colour selection is rife with stumbling blocks. Just how effectively can a diverse passenger universe relate to individual colours? For example, in Western cultures black is generally associated with funerals and bridegrooms, while white is traditionally worn by the bride on her wedding day – a happy occasion, presumably. Yet in some regions of the Far East, brides wear dramatic red robes, while white is associated with funeral attire. In parts of Brazil, white is associated with energy, and in Japan it is the winning colour in opinion polls. But in Arctic regions white is regarded as the colour of extreme danger, associated with catastrophic whiteout weather conditions which could spell disaster in hostile terrain where there is no place to hide and no way to escape, say, a rapidly approaching polar bear searching for a tasty lunch.

In some countries, green represents change, hope, nature and growth, but in others it is the colour of jealousy, the green-eyed monster of Shakespeare's *Othello*. In the aviation world, green has traditionally been used as a 'house' colour by a number of airlines that fly for countries in Africa and in the Middle East and

Near East, and is also a key colour at Aer Lingus, Air Canada, Alitalia and Cathay Pacific. However, by far the most prevalent colour in aviation is blue, which has a long and proud history.

## BLUE NOTES

In Roman Britain, the arriving legions were awed by the ferocious, blue-coloured warriors who battled against them. According to Julius Caesar, in *Gallic War V 33*, 'All the Britons, indeed, dye themselves with woad which produces a blue colour, and makes their appearance in battle more terrible.' And, if Caesar had invaded India, what would he have said about Krishna, the indigo-skinned warrior deity of Hinduism? Both woad and indigo are colourants extracted from plants, following a complicated process of drying and fermenting. The ancients believed that these blue dyes could help to heal wounds and injuries sustained in battle.

In *Blue: The History of a Colour* (2001), Michel Pastoureau explains how blue became the entrenched favourite in Europe and America, surpassing all other colours in modern scientific-research

Courtesy Aer Lingus

Courtesy China Southern

*Blue is the most popular colour in aviation. Even the recently launched PrivatAir service is using navy-coloured leather seat covers (see Chapter 16/Ways Ahead). Blue was selected as a key colour for the computer-simulated aircraft-interior design scheme shown on the cover of this book*

*The choice of red as a key house colour signalled to the world that Virgin Atlantic was not cast in the mould of the old-style airlines (see Chapter 2/Business-Class Comfort and Chapter 12/The Leather Forecast)*

Courtesy Virgin Atlantic

programmes. And although it had been almost totally absent in ancient Western art and language, blue became classed as a 'moral colour' during medieval times, when it came to be associated with the worship of the Virgin Mary, who is frequently depicted wearing a blue dress or cloak. Later, blue became a significant royal colour, displacing the earlier reds that signalled bloodlines and inherited authority and the greens that were linked to hunting rights.

By the eighteenth century, the popularity of blue had spread across the government, the military and 'romantic' arenas. Since the French Revolution, when the clothes of the working class achieved preferential political status, blue has advanced steadily to become the colour of the people. In addition to the blue jeans and blue blazers now sold everywhere in the world, blue uniforms are the norm for employees in 'people jobs' (for example, police officers or attendants on buses, trains, ferries, at the theatre or in garages). Blue is the official colour of the UN and its predecessor, the League of Nations, of the United Nations Educational, Scientific and Cultural Organization (UNESCO) and the European Union (EU), and of many thousands of packaged products and brands, from 'Big Blue' (IBM)

to the recently established airlines jetBlue in the United States and Virgin Blue in Australia.

Aviation specialists may be extremely perturbed that Pastoureau's *Blue* does not mention aircraft interiors. Could the eagle-eyed author simply not have noticed that in the past 20 years airlines have spent literally billions of dollars on this colour? There has been a relentless phasing out of earth tones, reds and oranges, and almost invariably these have been replaced by blue-based schemes. And as of November 2001, even the British Airways Concorde started to fly a blue decor scheme.

And who can blame passengers for asking: Why do the pilots and flight attendants from so many different airlines all look almost the same in those dark blue outfits? In view of the airline industry's strong maritime heritage, it is not surprising that aircraft captains would wish to emulate ships' captains in their preference for dark blue uniforms. This is a reflection of the concept of the guild-type mentality of a specialist work force, where the strength of the bonds of brotherhood transcends the interests of individual employers. Today, however, customers say that the uniformity of this dress

*The rich orchid colours associated with the Thai heritage help create a cabin ambience of glamour and exotic allure*

code makes it difficult to tell which pilot belongs to which airline.

As for the cabin staff, in the early days of flying, their uniforms communicated their special job skills, such as those of stewards and nurses, for which they had been recruited by the emerging airlines. However, as the aviation business developed, these flight attendants fought battles with uniform-planning committees: they wanted to be seen as adjunct cockpit crew rather than as symbols of nursing, hosting and hospitality. The argument is that their primary role relates to safety on board the aircraft. Over the years, airlines worldwide have acceded to the wishes of their cabin crews, and blue is now the colour most frequently used for their uniforms.

Not surprisingly, the airlines have had to consider adding scarves, collars, cuffs, bows, belts, buttons and assorted details, in all the colours of the rainbow, to achieve even a minimum level of distinctiveness. Still, there are a few notable exceptions that have gone much further in helping to brighten up the airline world. For example, for nearly 30 years the softly smiling Singapore Airlines flight attendants have worn the uniquely coloured batik 'Sarong Kebaya' outfits (see Product Branding section) originally created by the Parisian designer Pierre Balmain. The memorable

colours of the Scottish tartan kilts of the British Caledonian cabin crew are still the stuff of high-flying legend, and at Thai International the exotic hues of the glorious silk gowns, sashes and fresh orchids worn by the glamorous flight attendants evoke fantasies associated with James Bond-type movies. Virgin Atlantic's decision, from the outset, to use the corporate 'Scarlet Lady' red for flight attendants' uniforms immediately marked the airline as a nontraditional enterprise, and the recent bold move by Delta to phase out its long-established dark blue uniforms in favour of dressing both male and female flight attendants in a combination of mid-grey and an unusual shade of periwinkle blue shows that a large airline can make use of a colour change to take a major step forward in the process of redefining its image.

**THE ROLE OF COLOUR**

There is a prevailing feeling that blue – and its cousin, blue-grey – is good for aviation. But do these colours generate more, or less, revenue for each airline? Are they easier to maintain than other colour combinations? Could it be that for certain nervous individuals a particular colour triggers an attack of air rage? And are

Courtesy easyJet

*The unusual orange decor scheme flown by easyJet is an expression of the airline's philosophy (as explained in this Chapter), 'For us, orange is more than just a colour . . . [it] is what makes us different'*

there colours that help make air travellers more relaxed? If so, what are these magic colours? Do they increase or decrease the chances of air rage? In addition, what role do colours play in inculcating customer and employee goodwill?

One forward-looking airline has tried to use colour as a way to 'jump out of the box'. From a start-up in 1995 with just two Boeing B737-200s sporting an exterior paint scheme in Day-Glo orange and white, easyJet rose to prominence in 2002 by becoming the largest low-cost carrier in Europe. On the occasion of being presented with the prestigious Award for Marketing by *Airline Business* magazine (August 2002), Chief Executive Ray Webster stated that the airline's famous orange logo is a key factor in its vision of its brand values: 'For us, orange is more than just a colour, it is a way of thinking. Orange is what makes us different.' EasyJet is unusual in that it does not sell its tickets through travel agents; more than 90 per cent of sales are via the Web. As Mike Cooper, Commercial Director, explained: 'We are offering something different from the past. The critical thing for us is to be recognized by as many people as possible. . . . We are not a faceless corporation.' Even in the foggy, rainy weather conditions that

are common at many times of the year in northern Europe, it would be extremely difficult to be unaware of the bright-orange presence of easyJet. The airline's look is akin to the corporate branding programmes associated with the dot-com generation: a youthful, consumer-friendly appearance.

Referring to the theories of Frank and Rudolf Mahnke, as stated in their work *Colour and Light in Man-Made Environments* (1993), the marketing design specialists at Lantal Textiles explain: 'Colour arouses definite emotional and aesthetic associations. The positive associations with blue are calm, sober, contemplative; the negative ones depressing, melancholy, cold. By contrast, the research showed that reds and oranges were linked with feelings of: strength, warmth and passion on the plus side; the negative associations are aggressive, intense and bloody!' They continue: 'Designers should incorporate this level of research into their basic decisions, in order to create fabrics that meet all the needs of the customer – including the physiological, psychological and aesthetic.'

The challenge for everyone working in the field of aircraft interiors is to achieve a balanced and unified look, one that is visually pleasing and, depending on the marketing requirements, brand appropriate. In the post-11 September 2001 operating environment, as airlines strive to realize cost savings and raise their average, year-round passenger-load factors, there will be an even greater need to evaluate the effects of colour, pattern and texture within the cabin environment to achieve improvements in the standards of aesthetics and maintenance. Now, more than ever, there is a need for objective research. Without a clear assessment of the risks and benefits that relate to specific colour choices, how can we justify moving ahead with a major investment of money, time and effort?

## COMMENTS FROM THE SPECIALISTS

### Philip George

*George Design Studio, Pine Plains, New York*
Has the romance of air travel ended? From the long-gone days of nurse-trained stewardesses through the glory days of the Pucci Braniff colour adventure to the greyed-down look of today, the perception of a dramatic, exciting voyage by air has been the hallmark of airline marketing programmes. The pressure of FAA safety mandates and the improved technology of airborne materials have not only resulted in safer and more user-friendly aircraft interiors today but may also provide the opportunity to break out of the grey mold.

The severe strains on carriers since 11 September 2001 will continue to change the dynamics of domestic air travel. The hub-and-spoke system that came about after deregulation will still permit small jets to service a wider selection of cities. Today, these smaller jets are used extensively as commuter and feeder services for major carriers to hubs. As these smaller aircraft carriers come into service and become competitive, I see an opportunity for some carriers to move from the greyed-down look to a more colour-sensitive cabin environment. The reduction or elimination of in-flight services and amenities provides an opportunity to re-examine the aircraft interior look utilizing new technologies, marketing, design, and safety and security considerations. It costs the same to create a low-maintenance, attractive, comfortable, serviceable and interesting interior of a small jet as it does to outfit an all-grey utilitarian one.

### Peter A van der Meulen

*Human Factors Engineer, Tecmath of North America, Inc, Troy, Michigan*
Great attention is given to cabin colour schemes, to manipulate passengers' perceptions of space, safety and luxury. These colour schemes primarily affect a passenger's subconscious sense of well-being. Although they influence passengers' emotions and behaviour, they do not send direct messages requiring immediate attention or action from passengers. An aircraft cabin also sends many visual messages to passengers that do require immediate attention or action – exit signs, seat numbers, 'Fasten Seat Belt' signs and emergency instructions. The colour of a visual message contributes significantly to its efficacy, in terms of quick perception and correct interpretation.

Everyone associates red with an emergency and green with a safe condition; thus an emergency-exit sign is usually red. An important factor in the ability of a message to draw attention to itself is the degree to which it stands out in its environment. Cabin lightning is often white, as are most illuminated messages. In addition, light coming in through windows is primarily white. So, for an illuminated message to stand out and attract attention, a colour other than white might be more effective. Car manufacturers use blue or green instrument-panel illumination, so that information stands out among the fast-moving white and red lights on a freeway at night.

Colours behave differently against different backgrounds. For example, the human eye cannot easily perceive a blue message on a red background. A red text on a black background stands out better than on any other background colour. During night flights, cabin lights are turned off. In low illumination, the human eye can perceive yellows and greens better than other colours.

Besides selecting appropriate colour schemes to affect passengers' well-being, designers should pay attention to effective use of colours for messages and signals in cabins, to improve safety and ergonomic qualities.

### Michael Clark Toomey

*Principal/Creative Director, Toomey Design Group, Inc, New York*
The two most popular colours for corporate identity in America are blue and red. The common perception is that blue is solid and reliable, while red may be bolder, more outgoing. This is a generalization but the point is that these are most people's perceptions of those colours. Colour has traditionally been selected based on aesthetic taste and on the attributes associated with a colour. The ability to reproduce colour has also been a factor. Today's technology has a bigger impact on choice. Historically, the cost of printing was a large factor in limiting choice for printed collateral, stationery or magazine ads. Now television, computer screens and the Web, as well as digital and conventional printing methods, all offer full colour at lower costs. Even many home-computer printers are full colour.

We can select and control colour around the world by using standardization language or specifications for printing inks from colour-specification systems such as Pantone, Trumatch, Focoltone and Toyo. There are colour chips for fabrics and plastics, as well as for paper, ink and computer screens, that can be identified by standardized, recognizable numbers.

With computer-controlled jacquard-style weaving machines, custom patterns and colours for fabrics and carpets can be developed. We can print and manufacture proprietary colour schemes for other surfaces to create interior elements that specifically relate back to the individual company's brand and look.

Marketing-savvy companies try to extend their identity and palette further through an ever more comprehensive list of communications applications, including print collateral, advertising, packaging, physical facilities and vehicles. Variations of the logo's colours are reinterpreted into related colour schemes appropriate to fabric for uniforms, seating upholstery or other surface applications. In the aviation sector there is still ample room to make an impact with colour and to extend brand identity with meaningful colour variations and patterns. Colour transcends language.

# Which Blue Seat Belongs to Which Airline?

## Answers
1-D; 2-G; 3-A; 4-E; 5-C; 6-H; 7-F; 8-B

Courtesy Iberia; Mexicana; South African Airways; Singapore Airlines; Yemenia

Courtesy British Airways

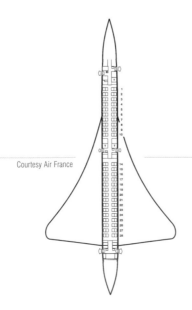

Courtesy Air France

Courtesy British Airways

# Chapter 14
## CONCORDE UNIQUE

*A Concorde fly-past is considered to be one of the most thrilling moments in the entire aviation experience. Although Concorde is now being withdrawn from service, we have retained this Chapter in its original format. It is intended as a tribute to all those who worked on the development of this legendary aircraft and presents a detailed memoir: how it feels to fly in the only supersonic salon in the sky.*

At the grand finale of the Queen's Golden Jubilee celebrations in 2002, more than a million revellers packed the streets of central London, each appearing to immediately recognize the beautiful, delta-winged shape of Concorde as it roared overhead. But how many of those spectators would immediately recognize the *interior* of Concorde? What does it look like? And how does it feel to live the high life 10 miles up?

Traditionally, the advertising programmes in both France and the UK have focused on the amazing outline of the fuselage of the world's only supersonic passenger aircraft. The interior of this flying miracle, however, is far more conventional. When Concorde was introduced into commercial service in 1976, passenger comments most often focused on the lack of space in the cabin, or that it was much smaller than they had expected. And even today, as you board the aircraft, the first words from the flight attendants are likely to be '*Attention à la tête, s'il vous plaît!*', or 'Mind your head, please!' The entryway door, located just behind the 'needle-nose' cockpit area, is smaller than those of today's commercial jets; average-size North Atlantic business travellers have to bow their heads on entering the cabin – as if they were at the portals of a temple, and were required to demonstrate fealty to this peerless Goddess of the Skies.

### THE SUPERSONIC SALON IN THE SKY

Concorde has two cabins, at the front and the rear, seating 40 and 60 passengers respectively. Lavatories and galleys are located behind the cockpit and between the cabins. And the seats are configured at a 37-inch (93.98-centimetre) pitch, and positioned in a 2+2 layout, that is, two passengers sitting next to each other, on each side of the aisle. The overall effect is streamlined and non-fussy. Although there is less space than in the business-class cabins of subsonic transatlantic aircraft, the length of time spent on board is considerably shorter, so passenger discomfort is rare. Some people describe the general feeling of being on board Concorde as comparable to that of sitting at a restaurant table for dinner or attending a theatre performance.

The flying time to New York from Paris or London is about three and a half hours, so with the five-hour time difference passengers 'arrive before they leave'. Hence its nickname of the 'Time Machine'. Passengers who are new to Concorde often ask whether it will be an exhausting experience to fly at about twice the speed of sound, and at twice the height of Mount Everest. Concorde regulars, however, are quick to explain that a supersonic flight in many ways resembles a half-day trip in an ultra-luxurious land vehicle or super-yacht. 'Many passengers were disappointed with the space provided, compared with a Boeing B747,' said Gerry Draper who, as Marketing Director at British Airways, headed the commercial development of Concorde. 'We therefore claimed that the experience was similar to an E-Type Jaguar, compared with a Rolls-Royce.'

But what about the employees? 'To make the Concorde crews feel special,' Gerry Draper explained, 'we commissioned the Queen's couturier, Hardy Amies, to design a distinctive, executive-style grey uniform for the flight attendants. The aim was to develop a Concorde cabin ambience that would be special and different from that normally experienced by passengers who were accustomed to flying on subsonic services.'

The vertical cross-section of the supersonic passenger cabin is not very different from that of today's 50-seat regional jets; that is, there is just enough room, in general terms, for adult passengers to walk along the aisle comfortably, with a few inches of clearance above the head. At a width of 16 inches (40.64 centimetres), however, the Concorde aisle might be a rather tight fit for anyone who is larger than average. The overhead stowage bins can accommodate small briefcases and carry-on luggage, but space for the big, rolling suitcases passengers bring on board larger aircraft is insufficient. It is hard to remember that, in the early days of service, the Concorde bins were even shallower, offering just

Courtesy Air France

*LEFT: In the Air France Concorde cabin design scheme, small-scale dark blue triangles appear as a decorative motif, e.g., on the aisle carpet (shown above). The sloping lines of the triangles link directly with the blue element of the airline's corporate logo, positioned at a slanted angle to indicate forward movement (as displayed on the tail fin of the Air France Concorde shown in this Chapter and in Chapter4/Aero Identity). In turn, the combination of the three colours displayed on the airline's tail fins derives from the blue, white and red tricolour which appears positioned vertically on the French national flag RIGHT: The windows of Concorde are very small. The 'bezel-shape' surrounds have been contoured to give the impression of larger overall dimensions*

enough capacity to hold a thin document portfolio and a bowler hat. During the pre-flight boarding routine, when customer service agents offered to stow bulky items in a 'special closet', passengers happily handed over fancy fur coats, reptile-skin attache cases, Ascot finery and fat rolls of documents labelled 'Strictly Confidential'. But were they aware that their precious possessions might be stowed in cargo hold number 5? (On arrival at the destination airport, these stowed items were given priority on the jetway bridge, to be reunited with their owners as if by magic!).

Although some sales brochures explained that the Concorde cabin would stretch by approximately 7 to 10 inches (17.78 to 25.40 centimetres) during the flight due to heating of the airframe, they neglected to inform passengers that because of this stretching, the bi-fold doors of some of the lavatories were prone to getting stuck, particularly during the mid-Atlantic section of the journey. Invariably, it seemed that the grandest titled names were the ones who got trapped, and noisy dramas ensued. An early solution to this problem was to reduce the vertical measurement of the door panels, to ensure smooth clearance within the door-frame aperture.

Another Concorde conundrum was that of the mysteriously shrinking carpet! Imperceptibly, the carpet would inch back from the rear-facing front wall and creep toward the toes of the unsuspecting passengers seated in the first row of the cabin. As the bare flooring started to reveal itself there would be heated debates

as to whether too much champagne had been imbibed. Eventually the ground crews refined the installation procedures and established a way to stop the directional 'pull movement' from dragging the first few inches of carpet toward the back of the aircraft.

The panes of the windows on Concorde are smaller than those of modern commercial aircraft. The measurement from top to bottom is about one adult hand span – approximately the stretch of an octave interval on a piano keyboard. However, the carefully structured contours of the window frame, and the positioning of the pull-down window shade – at 4 inches (10.16 centimetres) in front of the actual window pane – help to create the impression of greater overall dimensions and act to offset possible feelings of claustrophobia. Many regular passengers like to sit next to the windows because, when the aircraft reaches its cruising altitude, they can get a unique view of the curvature of the earth and can see the unforgettable indigo shading of the horizon. The impact of this mind-opening visual experience, coupled with the fact that flights are almost turbulence-free and the swooshing sounds of the engines can be soothing, are among the reasons given by passengers for their feelings of well-being when they arrive at their destinations. Gerry Draper explains this further: 'We used to feature the cabin environment as "Like a Spring Morning", because the Concorde is the only airliner with a strong fuselage, enabling it to be pressurized to ground level. Hence you do not suffer from the oxygen starvation that builds up on subsonic flights, and makes a major contribution to jet lag.'

On a typical Concorde Atlantic crossing, on both scheduled and charter services, passengers are served a morning meal, lunch or dinner. The deluxe menus feature gourmet delicacies including caviar, tiger prawns, trout, fillet of beef, seasonal fresh fruits and handmade confectioneries, accompanied by renowned champagnes and wines – all presented on damask linen and the finest china. If they prefer, passengers can request a single-tray light meal incorporating a fresh fruit starter and a cold plate to allow more time for resting or working during the flight.

Add to this the excitement of the feeling of the slight 'push in the back' as the aircraft passes through Mach 1 and accelerates to Mach 2, twice the speed of sound, as displayed on the Machmeter located at the front of each cabin; the sheer glamour of being cocooned in the exclusive, club-like companionship of the great, the good and the unusual; and the indescribable thrill of having lifted off from the face of planet Earth to hurtle toward the edges of space, travelling faster than a rifle bullet!

### THE COST?

Critics point to the Concorde surcharge of about 20 per cent above the normal first-class fare. But paying about US$1000 extra to fly one way on Concorde is of absolutely no concern to top-level business executives whose companies operate on the principle of 'time is money'. When there was twice-daily service, some aficionados took the out-and-back trip within the day; in this way, they argued, they could avoid paying for costly hotel accommodation, and save a significant amount of money. Passengers can enjoy similar savings by making same-day connections at either end of their route.

### AIR FLAIR

To meet the expectations of this most elite of all market segments, there have been, over the years, many ingenious efforts

Courtesy British Airways

Courtesy British Airways

*In the British Airways Concorde cabin design scheme, which was used from 1985 to 2001, nearly a dozen nuanced shades of silvery-grey appeared in the leather-and-fabric seat covers, curtains, carpets, blankets and trim pieces. All accessory items and mementos were carefully calibrated to blend into the overall presentation. Subtle platinum banding, e.g., around the outer edges of the dining tableware, provided the finishing touch*

Courtesy British Airways

on the part of designers to create the impression of greater room-iness within the relatively cramped cabin dimensions. During the mid-1970s, for the Concorde proving flights, the test-aircraft flew a tan-coloured corporate-style decor scheme described by some enthusiasts as 'the Barbarella style' – referring to the voluptuous curves of the horizontal rolls of leather that cushioned the happy travellers. On the British Airways aircraft during the early years of commercial service, there was also a business-look theme, though this tended to be rather more precise, more 'Anglo-Saxon style', characterized by flat, horizontal stripes set in solid parallel lines across the seat backs.

In 1985, as part of the corporate-identity change that preceded the move to privatization, British Airways launched an exciting new decor scheme for its Concordes fleet. Designed by Landor Associates, the main feature was the use of an ultra-sophisticated combination of silvery-grey leather and a complementary 'limo fabric' wrapped around the central insert panel of the seat back.

The foams of the seats were resculptured to provide greater lumbar support – and to look and feel more rounded and streamlined – and the armrests were given extra padding. The overall styling was based on treatments associated with Lamborghini and Maserati super-luxury sports cars. Almost immediately, this new look became synonymous with high-end business, and in various parts of the world airlines began to install copycat grey seat covers.

During the mid-1990s, Air France introduced a new interior scheme on its Concorde fleet. Designed by Andrée Putman, this featured crisp, white, linen-style 'hoods' covering the top section of the seat backs – a classic treatment frequently seen in high-class restaurants or in the dining rooms of grand country mansions. The seats themselves were covered in grey. Small navy blue triangles were incorporated as a decorative motif on various accessories and to highlight the aisle lines of the carpet. (This motif has a distinguished provenance: the sloping line of the triangle shape accords directly with the navy blue element

*The white jacket worn by the cabin services director perfectly com-plements the white 'hoods' and pillow covers on the aircraft seats*

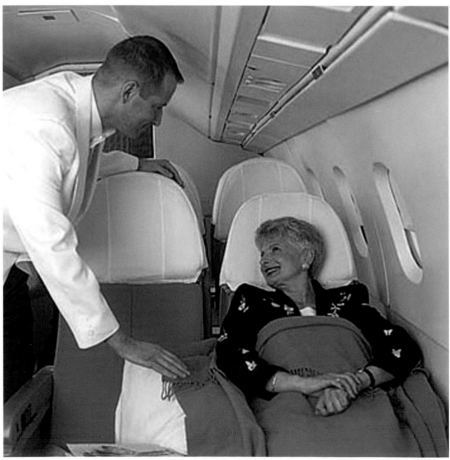

Courtesy Air France

Courtesy British Airways

of the Air France logo, which in turn derives from the graphic combination of the French national flag).

Diane Cornman, Manager, Corporate Communications, explains that Air France uses the Concorde image to promote concepts of French-style cuisine and technology: 'The exterior of the aircraft and its supersonic performance are certainly unique and well known. Inside the cabin we try to create an equally unique travel environment. For example, our flight attendants arrive at the airport wearing their standard uniforms. Before boarding the Concorde, they change into special ensembles that are compatible with the interior decor of the aircraft.

'The dining experience can be memorable despite the constraints of supersonic flight. In conjunction with Alain Ducasse we have run programmes that show French cuisine at its best. At the beginning of the millennium, Mr Ducasse prepared westbound lunch menus including foie gras, *canard confit* and

Brittany lobster with Osetra caviar. For eastbound brunch, the à la carte menu offered scrambled eggs with truffles, foie gras with truffles, and lobster with reduced tomato purée and truffles. Importantly, the Concorde crews also received half-day training courses in Alain Ducasse's kitchens to meet his high standards of service and presentation.

'At other times, French design has been featured through a series of menu covers designed by Christian Lacroix. The series was greatly appreciated and was offered to passengers as collectible items.'

## FLYING INTO THE FUTURE

There was an initial outburst of enthusiasm and admiration when in spring 2001 Boeing unveiled its plans to build a new aircraft called the Sonic Cruiser. The diagram on the drawing board, enticingly futuristic, immediately evoked comparisons with Concorde, and

Courtesy Air France

*The crème-de-la-crème clientele of Concorde deserves the very best that the aviation world can offer! As described in this Chapter, the Air France Concorde has featured menus prepared by the celebrated French chef Alain Ducasse and these menu covers designed by the haut couturier Christian Lacroix*

many travellers around the world began to ponder the implications of transferring their loyalty to a new, wide-bodied Goddess of the Skies. Sadly, this twin-aisled deity did not transcend the drawing-board, so Concorde's supremacy remains unchallenged.

Although it was developed decades ago, the Concorde look is still considered the height of fashion. For example, in the US, when the carrier jetBlue commenced operations flying an all-new single-aircraft-type fleet, it proudly advertised grey all-leather seat covers from the nose to the tail of the Airbus A320 – for a low-cost, low-fare, all-one-class, no-frills service.

In 2001, the year the fleet was grounded for necessary safety modifications, the budget for the British Airways Concorde interior-upgrade programme was US$21 million. This scheme was designed by Factory, working with Sir Terence Conran. Discreetly opulent, the new seats are contoured to include a cradle mechanism, a new footrest, an adjustable headrest and easier access to the seat-recline and in-flight entertainment control pad. In addition, a small amount of under-seat stowage space has become available. The latest leather seat covers are a purplish blue, a powerful shade inspired, possibly, by the awe-inspiring colour on the planetary horizon line. There are also matching glossy leather 'bumper' surrounds on the drop-down extendable meal tray-tables.

Once again we see stripes in action. On the carpet, as an integral element of the grey scheme, there was previously a red Speedwing line running from the nose to the tail of the aircraft, down the aisle, close to the lines of the seats. This has been

Courtesy British Airways

replaced with transverse stripes running from one side of the cabin to the other. There is now a new Concorde blanket in a pale creamy colour, made from ultra-fine fabric, which folds as small as a pashmina shawl; its pattern displays elegant stripes in a reverse version of those on the carpet. The pale colour has also been used for the curtains, and for the flat leather-finish panelling treatment that appears on the cabin dividers.

Although there has been no move to install in-seat power-supply outlets, movie screens or individual TV sets, the general consensus is that this new-millennium approach is well up to the superlative standards originally envisioned by the Concorde pioneers.

## COMMENTS FROM THE SPECIALISTS

### Barbara Bermack
*Travel Consultant, Mercury International Travel, New York*
The cost of travelling on Concorde is out of reach for most of my clients, since corporate policies restrict even upper-echelon

employees to flying business class when travelling overseas. For those few clients who are fortunate enough to fly on Concorde, comfort is not the factor that drives their desire to consistently choose this aircraft. The speed and the time that it saves more than make up for the cost when standard transatlantic business travel can keep them in the air for so many hours. These clients are not interested in sleeper seats, sight-seeing and dining in foreign cities, and will not even notice the weather conditions when they reach their destination. It's get on, get there, get off, take care of business and return home as quickly as possible.

Time is money indeed. Whether clients want to return quickly to be with their families or to be back in their own offices, time spent travelling is perceived as wasted time. Concorde allows my travellers the best of both worlds. When the Concordes were taken out of service, my clients went through a period of withdrawal. When they were brought back into service, my loyal Concorde travellers booked three or four trips at a time. They were just so glad to be able to control a little more of their lives.

*The new British Airways Concorde cabin design scheme features shades of indigo, beige and off-white. Glove-soft leather is used for the seat covers, tray-table surrounds, seat-back literature pockets and the panelling treatment on the cabin dividers. The genius pioneers of Concorde would certainly have been impressed!*

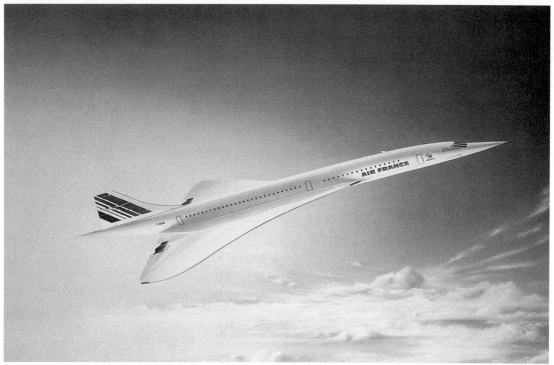

Courtesy Air France

Concorde clients are the best-travelled in the world. They understand that they sacrifice the luxury of first-class sleeper seats and spacious cabins to fly on this aircraft. They wouldn't have it any other way.

**Richard Stein**

*CEO and Executive Creative Director, Enterprise IG Japan, Tokyo, Japan*

When we were awarded the Concorde interior project, in 1985, and surveyed the square seating and traditional brown striped fabrics, our immediate impression was that the interior did not emphasize the speed and grace of the exterior silhouette. We were told that the original scheme was developed because the airline felt that travellers on Concorde might be afraid to fly at supersonic speed, so the interior was made to emulate a Pall Mall gentlemen's club.

For the new look, our opinion was that the interior should more closely reflect the shape of the fuselage. We redesigned the seats more along the lines of a luxury sports car and reduced the bulk of the backs by introducing a more curvilinear, body-hugging shape. The seats were removed from the aircraft and rebuilt in a workshop near Heathrow Airport, where they were 'sculpted' into a shape that both we and British Airways liked. Everyone was pleased – that is, until the time came to reinstall them and we found that they wouldn't fit through Concorde's small door! Everything had to be disassembled and rebuilt inside the aircraft, though in the end I believe everyone agreed it was worth it.

**THE AVIATION LEGEND**

In 2003, both Air France and British Airways announced that Concorde would be withdrawn from service, for economic reasons. All faithful followers of Concorde were devastated to hear this news. If, as suggested, some of the aircraft become walk-through museum exhibits offering virtual flights, the supersonic jetliner cabin design could be experienced and enjoyed by many more people on the ground than ever flew in Concorde during her 27 years of fame.

Concorde passengers will always remember the fighter-like climb, the acceleration through Mach 1 and the first sight of the curvature of the earth under a deep blue sky. Future generations will continue to be inspired by the visual impact of this wonderful aircraft. The Concorde legend could live for ever.

'Flying with a Happy Face.' Over the years at Alaska Airlines, 'The Smiling Eskimo' (see opposite) has witnessed major cabin upgrades including the hotel-style, full-service, stand-up cocktail bar and the sit-down panoramic viewing lounge (note rear-facing seats) complete with decorative depictions of local wildlife

# Chapter 15
## UPGRADES
### Refurbishing Aloft

*Some people cite the 'house-renovation rule' that 'It'll cost twice as much –
and take three times as long – as you first thought it would.' Others say that
upgrades constitute the primrose path that will eventually lead to true product
perfection. Strictly mandated regulatory requirements govern all stages of the
decision-making process.*

To provide a competitive standard of customer service, to add value to the brand positioning and meet heightened safety and security requirements, it is necessary to constantly review and redefine the in-flight product experience. At almost any time, most airlines are involved in some kind of upgrade or refurbishment programme. In recent years, many of these have been widely publicized, including those that have strengthened cockpit doors, increased the amount of space adjacent to the emergency-exit doors and brought seats into compliance for the new 16g standard (see later in this Chapter).

Another area of activity – but one that might be less obvious to passengers – is the steady upgrading of crew rest accommodation. As modern aircraft fly ever-longer stage lengths, and as labour contracts consolidate the precise details relating to rest periods for crew members, there is a need to provide more than the old-style 'sardine row' of heavy fabric curtains on the main deck behind which crew members could take a quick nap. At United, on the Boeing B747, the 'crew bunk house' is located in the aft area of the aircraft, above the main cabin, between the ceiling and the exterior contour of the aft fuselage. At South African Airways, on the same aircraft type, the crew rest area is located above the ceiling panels at the rear of the upper deck. In each case, employees have to climb a few steps to reach their dormitory accommodation, and say that this is a bit like using the attic of a house: the space has always been there, but traditionally it hasn't been utilized.

### AESTHETICS AND PRACTICABILITY

Partial upgrade and refurbishment plans can look good on paper, but in reality someone has to ensure that an aircraft's new on-board supply stocks are going to be compatible with the existing schemes. Many different issues need to be studied in detail before the money is spent, for example appearance, colour, texture, size and scale of patterning, cleaning cycles, storage requirements, life expectancy; the number of times that an item can be used, the length of time required to physically handle the items at the time of installation, and ease of installation via a specialist or a nonspecialist.

Courtesy Alaska Airlines

## BEING THRIFTY

Passengers are aware of the visible enhancements associated with modernizing the aircraft interior – new seats, larger baggage stowage bins, power-supply outlets for laptop computers and the like. For the airlines, however, the short-term and long-term cost implications of all these programmes have to be studied in great detail. At the same time as they start to install seat-back TV sets, airlines might cut back in areas that are less conspicuous, for example: removing the sprig of parsley from all economy-class lunches and dinners for a year; changing from traditional cloth headrest covers to a disposable paper version in a smaller size; flying blankets and pillows that are thinner and lighter-weight – making them not just cheaper to buy but a way to reduce the year-round fuel-burn figures; reducing the selection of wines and spirits; launching joint-sponsorship deals with well-known retail brands to cover the provision of coffee and soft drinks; offering pretzels and chips instead of the traditional meal service; using a tougher fabric for seat covers that will stand up to more washings; reconfiguring the cabin to jam in more revenue-generating seat rows, consequently decreasing seat pitch; abandoning unprofitable routes; and flying smaller aircraft in order to reduce operating costs.

## FLAMMABILITY AND STRUCTURAL CERTIFICATION

At all stages of the planning cycle, it is necessary to take into account the significant issues relating to Federal Aviation Administration (FAA) flammability and structural certification. Bill Rathmanner, President (FAA Designated Engineering Representative) of Aero Design Services, Inc, explains: 'The

aircraft manufacture date can influence the flammability standard that the new materials must meet. Although it becomes less important as older aircraft are retired, aircraft manufactured prior to 20 August 1988 need not have the latest smoke-density and heat-release standard applied unless a "substantially complete replacement" of the interior is accomplished as defined by the FAA. Between that date and 20 August 1990, an interim standard for smoke density and heat release was applied until materials that could meet the desired standard were developed for aircraft manufactured after 20 August 1990. It is believed that the industry will eventually discontinue (if it hasn't already) the older materials in favour of the latest ones for manufacturing and inventory efficiency as well as for enhancing aviation safety.

'Also, when replacing fabric dress covers using the existing cushions, certification can be accomplished by similarity to previously approved tests when changes in dress covers result in the same material composition (plus or minus 6 per cent) and weight is essentially the same (lighter fabrics being more critical). However, a vertical burn-test comparison must also be made and the material must be shown to be equal to or better than the originally tested material. It may also be useful to evaluate the weight loss and burn length of the original "fire blocking" test.

'One of the structural issues to consider is the seat certification standard,' continues Bill Rathmanner. 'An aircraft that has FAR 25.562 in its certification basis must have the seats dynamically tested with anthropomorphic dummies (ATD) riding in the sled rapidly propelled and then slowed down to meet a very specific "16g" acceleration/deceleration curve. The seat must not

Courtesy Eastern Airlines

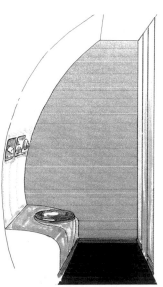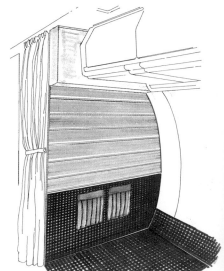

Courtesy Eastern Airlines

only remain structurally intact but human injury criteria must always be within specified limits. From the installation perspective, the seat cannot deform into specified passageways, assist spaces or aisles, and must not impede evacuation from the seat.

'And one must not forget to assess also the mechanical and electrical-systems implications, as well as aircraft performance and weight and balance considerations. It is always imperative that the airline or certification specialist communicate with the FAA Aircraft Certification Office early on for any major alteration and to avoid costly delays.'

## PLANNING THE NEW LOOK

Recalling major fleet-upgrade programmes during her time at United, Staff Representative Engineer, Cabin Interior and Exterior Livery Specialist, Alina Pham, outlines the key stages of the approval and certification process: 'First of all, the company's aircraft interior colour scheme needs to be defined. Designers have to create a scheme that will achieve pleasing aesthetic standards, as well as comply with certification and maintenance requirements. This means selecting colours through a subjective process and carrying out a thorough market-research programme involving a wide variety of internal and external organizations. The designers also have to meet with all those departments across the company that are going to be affected by the future changes. They have to seek input to ensure that the proposed colour scheme will be certifiable, acceptable and maintainable. Installation considerations are equally important in the approval process.

'The next step is to research and work with officially approved product suppliers and various teams to develop actual samples. These will need to be reviewed for exact matches to the size, shape, weight, colour, texture, thickness and feel of the design and product. To ensure consistency, all the products submitted need to be carefully inspected and reviewed using a specified light booth.'

So what happens after the samples have been selected? Alina Pham continues: 'The next stage is the testing process. One of the most critical areas is the mandatory flammability certification testing, as required by the FAA. Products must be tested and certified to ensure that they meet the stringent FAA flame-retardancy guidelines, as well as the smoke and toxicity requirements. These tests are performed in an approved FAA testing facility with a certified Designated Engineering Representative (DER) witnessing the test.

'In addition to the FAA testing, there is a rigorous programme of technical engineering testing covering durability, reliability, abrasion, colourfastness, stain resistance, shrinkage, dimensional stability, etc. All the tests relating to maintainability and consistency are essential in order to complete the approval process.'

Following the approvals and confirmations, Alina Pham concludes: 'The approved samples will then be produced at high-tech mills. Fabrics will be cut and sewn into seat covers. Carpets will be cut and serged into the required footprint shapes. Decorative laminates will be trimmed to cover areas such as sidewalls and ceiling panels. Plastics will be molded into parts. Placards will be tailored to size. The final production of all materials will need to be certified and will need to meet all established FAA and technical engineering testing on a continuous basis – meaning every production lot. Finally, the completed parts will be installed on the aircraft.'

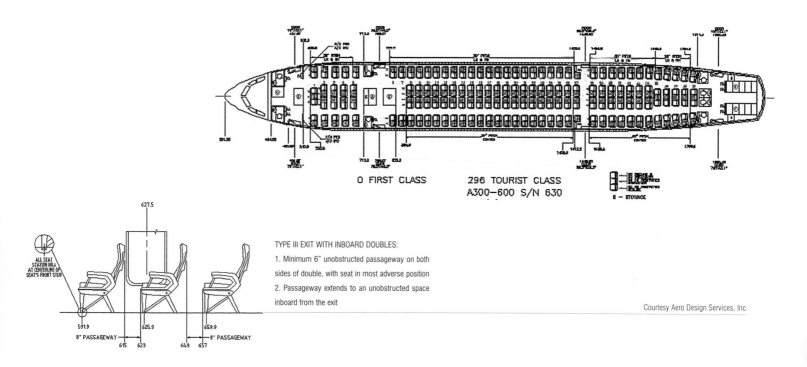

O FIRST CLASS          296 TOURIST CLASS
A300-600 S/N 630

TYPE III EXIT WITH INBOARD DOUBLES:
1. Minimum 6" unobstructed passageway on both sides of double, with seat in most adverse position
2. Passageway extends to an unobstructed space inboard from the exit

Courtesy Aero Design Services, Inc

## ANATOMY OF AN UPGRADE

The cost levels of upgrade and refurbishment programmes can vary enormously, because so many purchase contracts are quantity sensitive. In very general terms, however, there are four categories, ranging from the basic level – where there might be opportunities for cost savings or at the very least a change that would not incur greater overall cost outlay – to the large-budget levels, sometimes tens or even hundreds of millions of dollars, associated with implementing a completely new travel concept.

*Following are some of the main upgrade categories.*

### Level 1

Minor miscellaneous soft furnishings and accessories, including:

- headrest covers;
- pillows and pillow covers;
- blankets;
- curtains and tiebacks; and
- plastic and paper components of the food-and-beverage service – place mats, tray liners, napkins, etc.

Replacements and changes at this level can usually be achieved fairly smoothly. From the point of view of good financial house-keeping the aim, usually, is to use up all existing supplies before moving to the new items. The process of phasing out the old and phasing in the new needs to be handled with great care: supply stocks of the new items need to be standing by and ready for use *before* the last items from the old stocks have been absorbed by the operation.

The new items are sometimes launched immediately on a carrier's high-profile routes. However, if there is an experimental angle it can be advantageous to try out the new items on the lower-profile routes and gather some research feedback from the key market segments. The logistics department can plan to lock in the new and the old supply stocks to certain parts of the net-work, or for use on certain aircraft types. Although this might sound straightforward, the process can be fraught with practical difficulties. At the major airports on a carrier's route network, there is usually a full range of facilities in place to handle major changes. At the airports located away from the carrier's main bases, however, there may not be sufficient resources or the flex-ibility to run parallel systems during a refurbishment programme.

### Level 2

Upgrading and refurbishment at this level can include:

- seat-cover fabric;
- arm caps;
- seat-back literature pockets;
- bulkhead-mounted literature pockets;
- seat belts;
- seat-belt buckles;
- carpet;
- seat-track covers;
- nontextile hard floor covering;
- kick strips (heavy-duty plastic coverings installed from the floorboards up to ankle level to protect areas likely to suffer from being kicked);
- bump strips (surface-mounted protective coverings in heavy-duty plastic or vinyl);
- bin strips (which run along the edge of the overhead baggage storage bins);
- placards and seat/row numbers;
- dado-panel treatments, for example carpet-type or gros-point-type fabric covering, high-tech paint, decorative plastic finish or laminates;
- decorative surface treatment for cabin dividers;
- doormats;
- flight-deck floor covering;
- flight attendants' seat covers and safety harnesses;
- magazine racks;
- baby bassinets; and
- china, glass and metal components of the range of food-and-beverage-service equipment – plates, cups, glasses, cutlery, etc.

### Level 3

Upgrades at Levels 3 and 4 represent an enormous investment and commitment on the part of the airlines that are able to mount such programmes, and refurbishments may focus on the following areas:

- seat foams;
- new seats;
- new seating layouts;
- hard plastics – seat side panels, tray-tables;
- vertical surfaces – cabin dividers, aisle and corridor treatments, sidewall panels;
- window shades;
- door liners and surrounds;
- coat closets; and
- 'dog box' storage units, consoles and bar units.

### Level 4

- galleys;
- lavatories;
- ceiling panels;
- overhead bins;
- entryway areas;
- cabin lighting systems;
- illuminated signs;

Courtesy Japan Airlines

- in-flight entertainment systems;
- audio channels, TV, video, power-supply outlets, tele-phones, computers, fax machines, etc; and
- new travel concepts, for example reconfiguration, shower facilities, private dressing rooms, welcome bars and crew rest dormitories.

## UPGRADE IN JAPAN

In a recent upgrade of its first-class cabin, Japan Airlines intro-duced into service its new Skysleeper Solo, a dreamy pale-coloured ovoid creation the design motif of which is taken from beautiful organic shapes and curves as found in the natural world. According to the sales brochure: 'The seat design's top priority is comfort and relaxation, both physically and mentally.' When reclined in the full flat position, the seat width is 26 inches (66.04 centimetres) and the length is 73 inches (1.85 metres). The con-tours of the table and the counter are curved, there is soft light-ing within the private space, and reading lights are set on both sides of the seat to avoid shadows. By decreasing the number of seats from 12 to 11, the airline has provided a more spacious cabin layout. Describing the individual compartments, which were designed by Ross Lovegrove, the company states: 'More than an evolution of seating, it is a revolution in rest, making passengers feel like they are one with their environment.'

## AND 'DOWN UNDER' IN AUSTRALIA

Preparing for a relaunch of its international business class, at an estimated cost of US$300 million, Qantas recently announced details of the planned product features. These include seats mea-suring 78 inches (1.98 metres) in length and 25 inches (63.50 centimetres) in width when fully reclined; a fixed cocoon surround to provide privacy and insulation against cabin noise; extensive adjustment control to ensure maximum comfort in any position for all customers, regardless of their height; stowage options for reading materials and other possessions, including a shoe cup-board and a glove box for spectacles and travel documents; a power-supply outlet that allows laptops to be plugged in without the need for adapter cables; a 10.4-inch (26.42-centimetre) TV screen offering multi-channel entertainment; a back-massage fea-ture; high-quality noise-cancellation headsets; new lighting sys-tems; a self-service bar area; original artwork on display at the front of the cabin; and a new cabin configuration with 15 fewer seats than in the present setup, providing more space for each customer.

Massive upgrade programmes of the type described above usually have to be spread over a few years, depending on the size of the fleet and the way the airlines schedule the ground time of their aircraft. However, with the development of computer graphics it is now no longer necessary to run the planning meet-ings in mock-up studios or on board aircraft, as was the custom in

Courtesy Japan Airlines

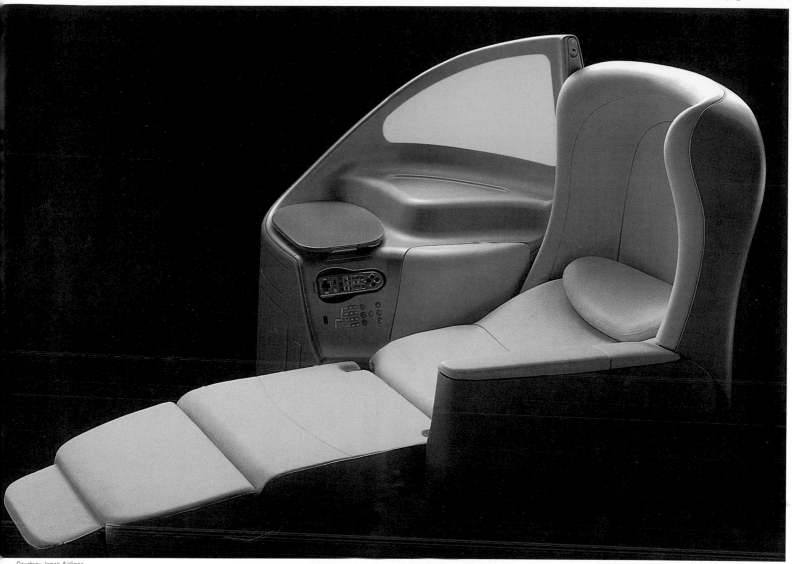

Courtesy Japan Airlines

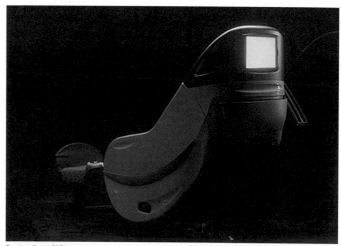

Courtesy Japan Airlines

Courtesy Airbus/Computergraphics ACA

previous decades. Peter Christoph Berg, Director, Computergraphics ACA GmbH, explains the process and the benefits: 'When there is a commitment to a major programme, computer graphics can greatly help the airline, the seat designers and the manufacturers to visualize a range of possible scenarios and to track the progress of various individual projects. For example, in the late 1990s, working with Swissair on its then state-of-the-art first-class seat, we were able, through computer simulations, to give the designers and the airline management an advance picture of the ways in which the different parts could be fitted together. As a result of this process they were able to assess the options and make key decisions before the technical drawings were finalized (see Chapter 10/Durability).

'We can also simulate a walk through the aircraft. By using multimedia tools we can demonstrate in a timely and cost-effective way a comprehensive range of configurations, lighting conditions, seat functions, colours, textures and fabrics. Through a sophisticated process of interactive animation, customers can view their aircraft cabins from a wide range of perspectives and try out different ideas.

'Computer simulation is the tool of our time, replacing renderings, sketches, overlays, paintings and mock-ups. The computer graphics are accurate to a measurement of 1 millimetre. Cost and time envelopes are reduced and the overall service is improved – to the satisfaction of the customer.'

## THE MARKETING IMPERATIVE

All these upgrades and refurbishment programmes pose massive challenges for the airlines. There is a constant need to develop innovative products while at the same time retaining the familiar, well-received, tried-and-tested passenger amenities. In the cut-throat aviation business, there are no rewards for standing still. But though it is always exhilarating to plan these programmes, implementation can bring many problems for the unwary. All departments concerned need to be designated 'stakeholders'. Success will come only from vision, discipline, teamwork and wholehearted cooperation from all sides.

Courtesy Airbus/Computergraphics ACA

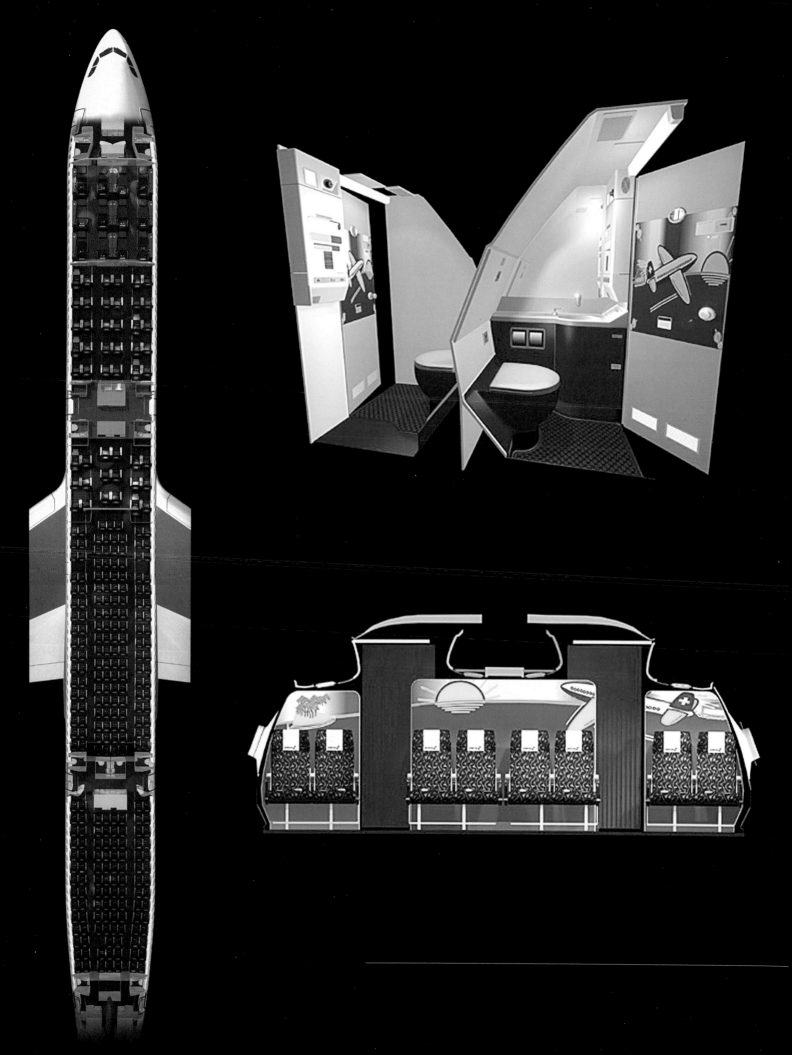

Courtesy Computergraphics ACA

## COMMENTS FROM THE SPECIALISTS

### Susan Henry

*Managing Director, Onboard Services and Catering, Northwest Airlines*

For refurbishment programmes, one of the key issues is proper testing, particularly with regard to such heavy-use items as seat fabric. Test companies with state-of-the-art facilities exist and should be used before approval of any fabric, no matter how attractive it may appear to the design team. There is nothing more frustrating than having a beautiful herringbone or brocade leave the hangar and have it quickly wear, fade and tear after only a few intensive trips. The costs of replacements are significant and frequent replacements add to the logistical limitations of the time budget for maintenance. No matter how beautiful the fabric, test and test it again.

### Marisa Infante

*Director, Marketing and Corporate Relations, Hoover Industries, Miami, Florida*

The greatest change that needs to take place in our industry is in the process for refurbishment and new image programmes. From the moment of design concept, we work with airlines on the selection of materials that are most appropriate to their aims for image and style and – very important – on the realistic maintainability and consistency (as well as the total cost) of the design. This has been an extremely successful way of avoiding the typical hit-or-miss approach of airlines when they independently select a design and materials and contact a sewing shop only at the last minute to get it all put together.

The dress coverings of aircraft are some of the most visible and vital elements of the cabin's appearance. They should be approached as a fine garment would be: find a designer you like and trust and a tailor who knows what he or she is doing, and leave it up to them to work out the details together. In the case of seat coverings, issues such as flammability requirements, certification to a particular seat structure and ultimately to the aircraft type, maintenance requirements and available manpower will be key in deciding, for example, whether cream really is the ideal cabin colour for an airline.

We recommend that a meeting of the airline stakeholders take place when the design image has either yet to be realized on paper or is no more than an artist's rendering. Ideally, representatives from the seat-structure manufacturer, designer and seat dress-cover manufacturer are present. This is the ideal time for brainstorming and addressing the issues of what is and is not desired as a result of this change. Once these issues have been ironed out up front, then it is a faster, more economical and less painful road to a successful image completion.

### Richard Stein

*CEO and Executive Creative Director, Enterprise IG Japan, Tokyo, Japan*

A comprehensive refurbishment programme can be a very cost-effective way to dramatically improve customer perception of airline quality. In a project we carried out for SAS, the airline refreshed a fleet of 79 aircraft by renewing every surface that the passenger came in contact with, or viewed, inside and out. This resulted in the perception that one was flying on a brand-new aircraft. This change was achieved for all 79 planes for less than the purchase cost of one new plane. The visual transformation was so complete and the airline so confident in its efforts that the press launch introducing the new livery and interiors was carried out using an aircraft that was, in fact, 14 years old.

As our work has evolved over the years, we have learned that it is very prudent and cost-saving in the long run to order new aircraft with cabins that feature relatively 'neutral' hard surfaces such as sidewalls, passageways and bulkheads. This allows quicker and less expensive interior scheme changes by focusing on the 'soft' furnishings, such as the seat covers, headrest covers, blankets and carpets. It is extremely difficult, time-consuming and expensive to replace cabin surfaces, and this often entails recertification of each component.

An additional benefit is that when an airline decides to sell one or more of its aircraft, potential buyers are more likely to favour cabins that will be easy to transform to their own colours and brand rather than ones that continue to carry telltale reminders of who owned them previously.

*One hundred years of progress!*

# Chapter 16
## WAYS AHEAD

*What about the jetliner cabins of the future? What will be the experiences of the next generation of airline passengers? What are the predictions for soon-to-be salons in the sky?*

At the beginning of the millennium, the International Air Transport Association (IATA) reported that:

- Aviation, the prime engine for travel and tourism, contributes more than US$3500 billion to the world economy, or nearly 12 per cent.
- Aviation helps support a tourist industry that employs 192 million people, 8 per cent of the world's total work force.
- Jet aircraft being produced today are about 70 per cent more fuel-efficient per passenger kilometre than those of 40 years ago.

With about 1.5 billion passengers flying annually, it would be reasonable to assume that the financial situation of most airlines is robustly healthy. The reality, however, is very different, and many airlines (including some of the largest) are in a financial state that can best be described as precarious.

### GENERATING CASH FLOW, BUT NOT PROFITS

There was a time when airlines belonged to shareholders to whom, at least in good years, they paid dividends. However this seems no more than a dream now. Toleration of high fixed costs has weakened the financial structure of many carriers to the point where they have fallen under the tyranny of the leasing companies and the fuel suppliers. Competition from nontraditional airlines and, most recently, the fall in passenger loads following terrorist attacks have brought many airlines to the brink.

The catastrophic fall in airline share prices might appear to be of interest only to shareholders who are, after all, inured to pain; but low share prices also threaten the necessary renewal of fleets. In the summer of 2002, financial reports showed the five biggest US airlines valued by the stock market at about 8 per cent of the value of their net fixed assets; it is hard to imagine that investors will put up new equity money when up to 92 per cent of it could vanish immediately.

This leaves only the financial institutions – primarily the banks – as a likely source of funds. But why should they be so imprudent as to finance loss-makers? Airlines in general are a poor way to make profits, though they do generate huge cash flows and a bank that has a satisfactory claim on the cash flow can be relaxed about lending. This leaves the airlines in a condition of marginal survival: still breathing yet subject to the continuation of life support from the banks, which are the real owners.

### PRODUCT PLANNING

Deregulation was supposed to increase competition. In practice, the world is now dominated by a small number of mega-carriers. Clearly, there is a pressing need for boutique products and niche marketing. At one level, the newspaper advertisements bombard their readership with pictures of snazzy little private jets, trumpeting the joys of charter, fractional ownership, hourly purchase and full ownership. (Warning: They usually fail to mention that many small aircraft are not equipped with lavatories – a fact that can come as a shock to passengers who are accustomed to the range of facilities offered by the scheduled airlines.) At another level there are outpourings of admiration for the plucky upstart carriers – for example Southwest and Virgin Atlantic – that have had the guts and the wherewithal to take on the majors. And, based on the successful model established by Southwest, other low-cost, low-fare, all-one-class, no-frills operators such as Ryanair, jetBlue and easyJet have already earned their place in aviation history, flying point to point on popular routes, using one aircraft type, with employees whose pay packets are far smaller than those of their counterparts at the traditional carriers.

In the meantime, the major airlines, in their battle to survive, have to display as much ingenuity as possible. Facing a classic conundrum, the age-old question of the 'long thin route', Lufthansa has adopted a new approach (see below). If the company can solve this problem, it will succeed in establishing a model that might be every bit as significant in the history of aviation as that of Southwest.

In most parts of the world, there are routes that do not always have a sufficient number of passengers to justify year-round operation. Background reasons for this include: seasonal traffic patterns; city pairs with insufficient market mass at one end of the route; predatory pricing by the competition; and loyalty to a national carrier operating alternative routings. Airlines can try to solve this problem by 'flying triangles', that is, by incorporating another point into the route pattern in one or both directions, or they might combine the flight with service to other cities, and fly a 'multi-sector route'. In addition, they might reduce frequency – for example operating three times a week instead of offering daily service, flying only during the high-traffic seasons, or combining some or all of the above 'solutions'.

Leisure travellers on 'long thin routes' are unlikely to complain about such scheduling shenanigans. Their travel arrangements are relatively flexible, and they are no doubt delighted to be offered the weekly 'Shock Announcement! All-Time Lowest Fares!' However, business travellers, who constitute the core market segment, are – understandably – not impressed. At each end of the route they are likely to make serious complaints to their corporate travel agents and, in an official capacity, to their local community business associations. Furthermore, they can threaten to divert future air-travel arrangements away from the offending carrier and toward the competition.

It was most heartening, therefore, to hear that finally someone somewhere was trying to develop the concept of niche product marketing, to offer a special service tailored to meet the needs of the long-suffering, long-haul, business-travel market segment.

## THE LUFTHANSA OPERATION

In June 2002 Lufthansa, in partnership with the Swiss VIP airline PrivatAir, launched an all-business-class service between Düsseldorf, Germany, and Newark Liberty International Airport, New Jersey, in the US. Flying daily, except Tuesdays, this is the only nonstop service from Düsseldorf to the New York area, and it is the first time that the German flag-carrier has marketed an exclusively business-class product of this kind.

The departure time from Düsseldorf is 10 am, with arrival at Newark at 12:30 pm local time, the same day. In the other direction, passengers depart Newark at 4:40 pm and arrive at Düsseldorf at 6:15 am local time, the next morning. With these timings, passengers have available to them a good range of connecting flights at both ends of the route.

Under a wetlease agreement (where the lease arrangement can cover an aircraft together with jet fuel and crew personnel) with Lufthansa, PrivatAir provides both the aircraft and the crew for this service: two flight-deck crew and four cabin crew. The 48-seat Boeing Business Jet (BBJ), based on a B737-700, offers an all-business-class seat configuration: 2+2 in 12 passenger rows.

### Passenger service standards

Aage Duenhaupt, Manager, International Communications, at Lufthansa Technik, AG, explains the floor-plan layout: 'The B/E Aerospace, cradle-type seats are configured at 55-inch [1.39 metre] pitch and recline to 145 degrees. The seat width is 19.7 inches [50.03 centimetres] and there is head and neck support, plus an adjustable footrest. There are three lavatories, one in the front of the cabin and two at the back. And so that guests are not disturbed while flight attendants are working in the aft galley, we have positioned a movable class divider behind Row 12.'

For in-flight entertainment, each passenger is offered a Sony Personal Video Watchman. As in the Lufthansa first-class cabins, passengers can create their own entertainment programmes, drawing from 15 movie titles, in up to 15 different languages, plus a range of music tapes.

Courtesy Lufthansa Technik AG & PrivatAir

Courtesy Lufthansa Technik AG & PrivatAir

## Style

The decor scheme has been carefully calibrated to ensure a professional ambience, suitable for travelling business executives. The main colours are deep blue and beige, with white accessories. The overall effect is streamlined and non-fussy – a successful formula given the constraints of a single-aisle aircraft. For example, the seat covers are dark-blue leather (not unlike the colour of those flying on the all-one-class Delta Shuttle or the British Airways Concorde). On each seat there is a classic white Lufthansa headrest cover, two white Lufthansa pillows and a blue Lufthansa blanket. The walls are light grey and the curtains and carpet are beige, the unusual striped pattern on the carpet adding a dash of character and individuality to the overall design scheme and drawing attention to the aisle, helping to give an impression of greater length and spaciousness.

## Meals

When meals are served, passengers open the tray-tables that are stowed in the armrest area of their seats. In addition to the scheduled meal service, passengers can ask to be served individually, at a time of their choosing. Special meals can be ordered in advance, when the flight reservations are made.

## Fares

No special surcharge is added to the fare. This exclusive business-class service is fully comparable to the business-class fares offered by Lufthansa on its mainline services.

## Baggage allowance

The baggage allowance is comparable to the usual Lufthansa business-class service on the airline's wide-body Airbus A340 aircraft: 30 kilograms (66.14 pounds) of checked baggage and two pieces of hand luggage.

## AIR TRAVEL OF THE FUTURE

The PrivatAir BBJ unit, which is locked into the Düsseldorf–Newark route, is not equipped with sky phones, power-supply outlets for laptop computers, conference tables, bars, business work stations, fax machines or shower baths, even though these high-tech features are provided by Lufthansa Technik for other VIP-BBJ programmes. However, if the Düsseldorf–Newark service turns out to be a success, business travellers of the future might find that they, too, will be able to enjoy the high-tech extra facilities that are currently associated with private aircraft owned by the super-rich.

At the old-style airlines, where there are prohibitively strong labour agreements in place, it might not be possible to offer wetlease arrangements of the PrivatAir type for a regular scheduled service. However, there is every chance that forward-looking airlines will be able to pick up an increasing amount of important niche traffic by offering a range of innovative products that are specially structured to appeal to passengers who wish to flee from the mass-transit herds.

In the new millennium, passengers are looking for more choices. Lufthansa deserves great success for displaying this initiative; its unique hybrid product is the result of blurring the boundaries between charter and scheduled operations, and it is to be hoped that this approach will usher in a vibrant new scenario for airlines, suppliers, vendors and manufacturers in both the charter and the commercial sectors of the industry.

A number of gloomy observers have opined that by offering this new service the airline may deprive itself of high-yield business traffic on its mainline services. They point to the fact that, many years ago, the plans for the dedicated luxury MGM service on certain US domestic routes did not work out. But the context is different today. Fewer major airlines are operating and, furthermore, airports have become much more of a problem to negotiate as a result of post-11 September 2001 security requirements; pushing through the huge crowds of people who are boarding, or disembarking from, an array of wide-body aircraft can be bad news for anyone's blood-pressure reading!

Business executives have a hard enough time anyway and, being the bread and butter of the airline world, they deserve as much ingenuity and creativity as the aviation specialists can dream up. As Aage Duenhaupt reminds us: 'You know, it's no problem waiting for your suitcases when there are only 47 other BBJ guests with you at the baggage carousel!'

Courtesy Lufthansa Technik AG & PrivatAir

Courtesy Airbus

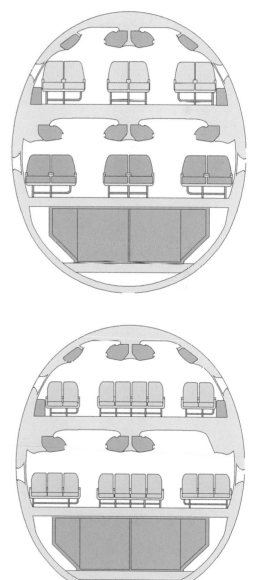

## THE BIG PICTURE

The prediction is that scheduled air traffic will triple over the next 20 years, and that by 2017 the annual increase in air travel will be greater than was total air travel in 1970, the year the Boeing B747 was launched. To cope with this predicted growth in air traffic, the number of aircraft in the world fleet is expected to double, to more than 30,000, by 2020.

Work is now proceeding apace on the 555-seat Airbus A380. It is said that future versions of this aircraft may carry up to a thousand passengers. Already, the world is agog to learn how the launch customers will decide to use the space available in the cabin. Libraries, shower units, coffee corners, dining rooms, lounge bars? So many options are available! However, exact descriptions of these future salons in the sky will have to be the subject of another study.

Courtesy Airbus

Courtesy Airbus

Courtesy Airbus

## FINALE

For the airline industry as a whole, though, times are still hard and it is difficult to see how or when they will change. It seems inevitable that sooner or later there will be a major reorganization and restructuring, and vast changes will be – will have to be – the result. Recreating what is now in many ways the world's biggest industry will be a Herculean task. We wait with bated breath, but in the meantime we shall continue to work to improve all the product features and customer benefits that passengers experience while flying above the clouds.

## CODA

The chapters of this book have examined the jetliner cabins of the world's commercial airlines from many different perspectives. In closing we should pay tribute to the commitment, skill and determination of all those aviation experts in all parts of the world whose work over the years has made this amazing business what it is today. This book is dedicated to each one of them. Finally, to the two visionaries from the bicycle shop who first flew at Kitty Hawk on 17 December 1903 …

thank you, Wilbur …

thank you, Orville.

*Courtesy Library of Congress*

*LEFT: Wilbur Wright, born 1867, near Milville, Indiana, US. Died 1912, Dayton, Ohio, US; RIGHT: Orville Wright, born 1871, Dayton. Died 1948, Dayton. The Wright Brothers, American inventors and aviation pioneers, achieved the first powered, sustained and controlled airplane flight on 17 December 1903 and opened the era of aviation*

# Bibliography

Anderson, David F and Eberhardt, Scott (2001) *Understanding Flight*, New York: McGraw-Hill

Anderson, John D, Jr (2001) *Fundamentals of Aerodynamics*, 3rd edition, Boston, Massachusetts: McGraw-Hill Higher Education

Ball, Philip (2002) *Bright Earth: Art and the Invention of Color*, New York: Farrar, Straus & Giroux

Bethune, Gordon and Huler, Scott (1998) *From Worst to First: Behind the Scenes of Continental's Remarkable Comeback*, New York: John Wiley & Sons

Bjone, Christian (2002) *First House: The Grid, the Figure, and the Void*, Chichester: John Wiley & Sons

Clegg, Brian (2002) *The Complete Flier's Handbook: The Essential Guide to Successful Air Travel*, London: Pan Macmillan

Craig, Gale M (1997) *Stop Abusing Bernoulli!: How Airplanes Really Fly*, Anderson, Indiana: Regenerative Press

Curtis, Eleanor (2001) *Hotel: Interior Structures*, Chichester: John Wiley & Sons

Endres, Gunter and Hewson, Robert (1996) *The Vital Guide to Major Airlines of the World*, Shrewsbury: Airlife Publishing, produced by Aerospace Publishing

Garfield, Simon (2001) *Mauve: How One Man Invented a Color That Changed the World*, New York: W W Norton

Gunston, Bill (ed) (1980) *The Illustrated Encyclopedia of Commercial Aircraft*, London: Phoebus Publishing

Hengi, B I (1997) *Airlines Worldwide: More Than 300 Airlines Described and Illustrated in Colour*, Leicester: Midland Publishing

Hersey, George (1999) *The Monumental Impulse: Architecture's Biological Roots*, Cambridge, Massachusetts: MIT Press

Jackson, Paul (ed) (1996/97) *Jane's All the World's Aircraft*, Coulsdon: Jane's Information Group

Lovegrove, Keith (2000) *Airline: Identity, Design and Culture*, New York: teNeues Publishing

Mahnke, Frank and Rudolf (1993) *Color and Light in Man-Made Environments*, New York: Van Nostrand Reinhold

Markham, Beryl (1983) *West with the Night*, San Francisco, California: North Point Press

Pastoureau, Michel (2001) *Blue: The History of a Color*, Princeton, New Jersey: Princeton University Press

Pina, Leslie A (1998) *Herman Miller: Interior Views*, Atglen, Pennsylvania: Schiffer Publishing

Simpson, Rod (1999) *Airlife's Commercial Aircraft and Airliners: A Guide to Postwar Commercial Aircraft Manufacturers and Their Aircraft*, Shrewsbury: Airlife Publishing

Spicer, Stuart (1997) *Dream Schemes: Exotic Airliner Art*, Shrewsbury: Airlife Publishing

Taylor, Michael J H (ed) (1996) *Jane's Encyclopedia of Aviation*, New York: Crescent Books

Tennekes, Henk (2000) *The Simple Science of Flight: From Insects to Jumbo Jets*, Cambridge, Massachusetts: MIT Press

Wall, Robert (1980) *Airliners*, London: William Collins Sons

Winters, Nancy (1997) *Man Flies: The Story of Alberto Santos-Dumont, Master of the Balloon*, Hopewell, New Jersey: Ecco Press

Zukowsky, John (ed) (1996) *Building for Air Travel: Architecture and Design for Commercial Aviation*, Chicago, Illinois: Art Institute of Chicago; Munich: Prestel-Verlag

Aviation Week (2003) *World Aviation Directory*, 2nd edition, Fall/Winter, Washington DC: Aviation Week

Aviation Week (2003) *World Aviation Directory's Buyer's Guide*, 2nd edition, Fall/Winter, Washington DC: Aviation Week

# Directory of Specialists

**Alg, Vern**
Senior Manager, Interiors Engineering,
Continental Airlines
13th Floor HQJIE, 600 Jefferson Street
Houston, TX 77002, USA
Tel: +1 (713) 324-8187
Fax: +1 (713) 324-7635
Email: valg@coair.com
www.continental.com

**Baron, Daniel**
Asia-Pacific Editor,
*Aircraft Interiors* magazine
Email: dbaron@gol.com
www.aircraft-interiors.net

**Berg, Peter Christoph**
Director, Computergraphics
ACA GmbH
Am Brand 4
82054 Sauerlach-Arget, Germany
Tel: +49 8104-668030
Fax: +49 8104-9208
Email: aca@aca-design.de
www.aca-design.de

**Bermack, Barbara**
Travel Consultant,
Mercury International Travel
630 Fifth Avenue, Suite 2207
New York, NY 10111, USA
Tel: +1 (212) 624-3620
Fax: +1 (212) 624-3636
Email: bbermack@merctravel.com
www.merctravel.com

**Bock, Thomas**
Director of Advanced Design,
Airbus Industrial Design, Airbus Central
1 Rond Point Maurice Bellonte
31707 Blagnac, France
Tel: +33 5 61 93 36 31
Fax: +33 5 61 93 38 74
Email: Thomas.bock@airbus.com
www.airbus.com

**Bogash, Richard R (Dick)**
Managing Director,
Sky Marketing Services, LLC
3406 SW 9th Street
Ft Lauderdale/Hollywood Airport
Ft Lauderdale, FL 33315, USA
Tel: +1 (954) 359-7797
Fax: +1 (954) 359-7749
www.skymarketingservicesLLC.com

**Boland, Michael M**
President and CEO,
Maritz Travel Company
2 Wheaton Point
Chesterfield, MO 63005, USA
Tel: +1 (636) 530-7575
Email: kelly0906@aol.com

**Boyd, James**
Public Relations Director, the
Americas, Singapore Airlines
5670 Wilshire Boulevard
Los Angeles, CA 90036, USA
Tel: +1 (323) 964-5185
Fax: +1 (323) 934-4482
Email:james_boyd@singaporeair.com.sg
www.singaporeair.com

**Bregman, Bob**
President, WESSCO International
1950 Sawtelle Boulevard #360
Los Angeles, CA 90025, USA
Tel: +1 (310) 477-4272
Fax: +1 (310) 477-7910
Email: bob@wessco.net
www.wessco.net

**Brown, Robert S**
Chief Executive Officer,
SYAIR Designs, LLC
PO Box 3441
Little Rock, AR 72203, USA
Tel: +1 (501) 537-7000
Fax: +1 (501) 537-7010
Email: bbrown@syairdesigns.com
www.syairdesigns.com

**Buck, Wendy**
Public Relations Manager,
Virgin Atlantic Airways
747 Belden Avenue
Norwalk, CT 06850, USA
Tel: +1 (203) 750-2000
Fax: +1 (203) 750-6430
www.virginatlantic.com

**Chown, Ford**
President, Linford Aerospace
Consulting Services, Inc
Formerly Chief Engineer Interiors,
Air Canada
307 Berkshire Avenue
Beaconsfield
Quebec H9W 1A6, Canada
Tel: +1 (514) 694-6165
Fax: +1 (514) 694-9947
Email: Linford_aero@videotron.ca

**Cornman, Diane**
Manager, Corporate Communications,
Air France
125 West 55th Street
New York, NY 10019, USA
Tel: +1 (212) 830-4000
Email: dicornman@airfrance.fr
www.airfrance.com/us

**Deignan, David**
Vice President, Operations, North
America, South African Airways
Terminal 3, JFK Airport
New York, NY 11430, USA

**Draper, Gerry**
Marketing Director at British Airways,
Managing Director for Intercontinental
Services at British Airways,
Chairman of Draper Associates
(Retired)
Fellow, British Chartered Institute of
Marketing
Awarded the OBE by Queen Elizabeth II
for services to aviation
76 Onslow Road
Walton on Thames
KT12 5AY, UK

**Duenhaupt, Aage**
Manager, International Communications,
Lufthansa Technik AG
Weg Beim Jaeger 193
22335 Hamburg, Germany
Tel: +49 40 5070 3143
Fax: +49 40 5070 8534
Email: aage.duenhaupt@lht.dlh.de
www.lufthansa-technik.com

**Ferrara, Ryan**
Manager, New Business
Development, Schneller, Inc
6019 Powdermill Road
Kent, OH 44240, USA
Tel: +1 (330) 676-7161
Fax: +1(330) 673-7327
Email: rferrara@schneller.com

**Gargano, Edward L**
President and CEO, MHM North
America
501 East 87th Street, Suite 2C
New York, NY 10028, USA
Tel: +1 (212) 772-7201
Fax: +1(212) 772-7355
Email: elgargano@aol.com

**George, Gail and Philip**
George Design Studio
1394 Route 83
Pine Plains, NY 12567, USA
Tel: +1 (518) 398-6668
Fax: +1(518) 398-6604
Email: gds8990@taconic.net

**Henry, Susan**
Managing Director, Onboard Services
and Catering, Northwest Airlines
7200 34th Avenue South
Minneapolis, MN 55450, USA
Tel: +1 (612) 726-7038
Fax: +1(612) 726-4768
Email: susan.henry@nwa.com

**Hooper, Stan**
Aviation Consultant
Formerly Interiors Engineering Director
Eastern Airlines
5035 NW 57th Way
Coral Springs, FL 33067, USA
Tel: +1 (954) 255-7551
Fax: +1(954) 255-7552
Email: aerostan@bellsouth.net

**Infante, Marisa**
Director, Marketing and Corporate
Relations, Hoover Industries
7260 NW 68 Street
Miami, FL 33166, USA
Tel: +1 (305) 888-9791 ext. 116
Fax: +1(305) 887-4632
Email: askmsahoover@aol.com
www.hooverindustries.com

**Jaffe, Steve**
Vice President and General Manager,
Bruce Industries
101 Evans Avenue
Dayton, NV 89403, USA
Tel: +1 (775) 246-0101
Fax: +1 (775) 246-0451
www.bruceind.com

**Jullies, Owen Graham**
Food and Beverage Manager,
Product Planning, South African
Airways
146A Johannesburg Road, Lyndhurst
Johannesburg, 2016
Republic of South Africa
Tel: +27 11 978 6006
Fax: +27 11 978 5835
Email: owenjullies@flysaa.com

**La Susa, Patrice**
Director, Commercial Aviation
Tapis Corporation
28 Kaysal Court
Armonk, NY 10504, USA
Tel: +1 (914) 273-2737
Fax: +1 (914) 273-2875
Email: patricelasusa@tapiscorp.com
www.tapiscorp.com

**Loschiavo, L J, Jr (Larry Lo)**
Vice President, SER-MAT
3104 South Andrews Avenue
Ft Lauderdale, FL 33316, USA
Tel: +1 (954) 525-1417
Fax: +1 (954) 525-1410
Email: sermat@mindspring.com

**Ludlum, Kenneth V**
President, Ludlum Products Company, Inc
603 Burns Lane
Winter Haven, FL 33884, USA
Tel: +1 (863) 325-8544
Fax: +1 (863) 325-8454
Email: k.v.ludlum@aol.com

**Luethi, Monika**
Director of Design, Department of
Development, Lantal Textiles
Dorfgasse 5
PO Box 1330
4901 Langenthal, Switzerland
Tel: +41 62 916 71 71
Fax: +41 62 923 25 32
Email: monika.luethi@lantal.ch
www.lantal.com

**Martin-Vegue, Phyllis**
Principal, and Director,
Interiors Studio, SMWM
989 Market Street
San Francisco, CA 94103, USA
Tel: +1 (415) 546-0400
Fax: +1 (415) 882-7098
Email: pmartin-vegue@smwm.com
www.smwm.com

**Moris, Lamberto G**
FAIA, Design Principal, SMWM
989 Market Street,
San Francisco, CA 94103, USA
Tel: +1 (415) 882-3003
Fax: +1 (415) 882-7098
Email: lmoris@smwm.com
www.smwm.com

**Ogawa, Alan J**
Vice President, Airport Operations
the Americas, Japan Airlines
300 Continental Boulevard, Suite 620
El Segundo, CA 90245, USA

**Peterson, Steve V**
Regional Sales Manager,
Douglass Interior Products, Inc
2251 North Rampart, #345
Las Vegas, NV 89128, USA
Tel: +1 (800) 804-5644
Fax: +1 (702) 255-6424
Email: svp@dipi.com
www.dipi.com

**Pham, Alina**
Aviation Consultant
Formerly Staff Representative
Engineer,
Cabin Interior and Exterior Livery
Specialist,
United Airlines
Email: phamalina@yahoo.com

**Raia, Jack**
Director, Modification Engineering and
DAS Administrator, Timco Engineered
Systems, Inc
623 Radar Road
Greensboro, NC 27410, USA
Tel: +1 (336) 668-4410 ext 3101
Fax: +1 (336) 662-8330
Email: raiaj@timcogso.com

**Rathmanner, Bill**
President, FAA DER,
Aero Design Services, Inc
6574 North State Road 7, Suite 114
Coconut Creek, FL 33073, USA
Tel: +1 (954) 346-0888
Fax: +1 (954) 346-0889
Email: aerobill@bellsouth.net
www.aero-design.com

**Rose, Jon**
Managing Director, MGR Foamtex Ltd
Unit 10/12 Jefferson Way
Thame, Oxon
OX9 3SZ, UK
Tel: +44 1844 260444
Fax: +44 1844 260157
Email: jon@mgrfoamtex.co.uk
www.mgrfoamtex.co.uk

**Ruffolo, Jeff**
Public Relations Manager,
China Southern Airlines
6300 Wilshire Boulevard
Los Angeles, CA 90048, USA
Tel: +1 (888) 338-8988
Fax: +1 (323) 653-8066
Email: ruffolopr@aol.com
www.cs-air.com/en

**Sandiford, David**
Manager, Aviation Sales, Mohawk
Industries, Inc, Aircraft Carpet Division
500 TownPark Lane, #400
Kennesaw, GA 30144, USA
Tel: +1 (678) 355-5796 or
        +1 (800) 554-6637 ext. 55796
Fax: +1 (678) 355-5812
Email:david_sandiford@mohawkind.com
www.mohawkair.com

**Sheahan, Peter**
Sheahan & Associates
42 Huntington Avenue
Scarsdale, NY 10583, USA
Tel: +1 (914) 722-6775
Email: psheahan@aol.com

**Sim, Stan**
Programme Manager,
Aerosud Interiors (Pty) Ltd
Cnr Van Ryneveld Avenue and Van Der
Sput Street
Pierre van Ryneveld, 0045
Republic of South Africa
Tel: +27 12 662 5043
Fax: +27 12 662 5169
Email: s.sim@aerosud.co.za
www.aerosud.co.za

**Stein, Richard**
CEO and Executive Creative Director,
Enterprise IG Japan
Humax Building
1-1-1 Ebisu-minami, Shibuya-ku
Tokyo 150-0022, Japan
Tel: +81 3 5768 4951
Fax: +81 3 5768 4952
Email: richard.stein@enterpriseig.com

**Toomey, Michael Clark**
Principal/Creative Director,
Toomey Design Group, Inc
345 West 88th Street
New York, NY 10024, USA
Tel: +1 (212) 877-5817
Fax: +1 (212) 877-5817
Email: toomeydesign@earthlink.net

**van der Meulen, Peter A**
Human Factors Engineer,
Tecmath of North America, Inc
1174 East Big Beaver Road
Troy, MI 48083, USA
Tel: +1 (248) 457-6820
Fax: +1 (248) 457-6824
Email: vdmeulen@tecmathna.com
www.tecmath.com

**Varley, John**
General Manager UK, Meridiana SpA
White Lodge, Cranbrook Road
Benenden, Kent
TN17 4EU, UK
Tel: +44 1580 240514
Email: varleyuk@aol.com

**Weiner, David Jay**
Architect
425 Park Avenue South, Suite 4C
New York, NY 10016, USA
Tel: +1 (212) 696-4345
Fax: +1 (212) 696-4384
Email: info@dweiner.com
www.dweiner.com

# Airline Websites

Adria Airways
www.adria.si

Aer Lingus plc
www.aerlingus.com

Aeroflot Russian
International Airlines
www.aeroflot.org

Aeromexico
www.aeromexico.com

Air Canada
www.aircanada.ca

Air France
www.airfrance.com

Air Kazakhstan
www.airkaz.com

Air New Zealand Ltd
www.airnz.com

Air Tanzania
www.airtanzania.com

Alaska Airlines, Inc
www.alaskaair.com

Alitalia SpA
www.alitalia.it

All Nippon Airways Co Ltd
(ANA)
www.ana.co.jp

American Airlines, Inc
www.aa.com

American Trans Air
www.ata.com

Asiana Airlines
www.asiana.co.kr

Austrian Airlines
www.aua.com

Avianca Airlines
www.avianca.co.uk

British Airways plc
www.britishairways.com

Brymon Airways Ltd
www.britishairways.com

BWIA International Airways Ltd
www.bwee.com

Cathay Pacific Airways Ltd
www.cathaypacific.com

China Southern Airlines Co Ltd
www.cs-air.com/en

Continental Airlines, Inc
www.continental.com

Delta Air Lines, Inc
www.delta.com

easyJet Airline Co Ltd
www.easyjet.com

El Al Israel Airlines Ltd
www.elal.co.il

Emirates Airline
www.emirates.com

Gulf Air Co, GSC
www.gulfairco.com

Hawaiian Airlines, Inc
www.hawaiianair.com

Iberia Airlines
www.iberia.com

Indian Airlines
www.indian-airlines.nic.in

Japan Airlines
www.jal.co.jp

Jet Airways
www.jetairways.com

jetBlue Airways
www.jetblue.com

KLM Royal Dutch Airlines
www.klm.com

Korean Air
www.koreanair.com

LanChile
www.lanchile.com

Lufthansa German Airlines
www.lufthansa.com

Meridiana SpA
www.meridiana.it

Mesa Airlines, Inc
www.mesa-air.com

Mexicana Airlines
www.mexicana.com

Middle East Airlines/Air Liban SA
www.mea.com.lb

Northwest Airlines, Inc
www.nwa.com

Philippine Airlines, Inc
www.philippineair.com

PrivatAir
www.privatair.com

Qantas Airways Ltd
www.qantas.com.au

Ryanair
www.ryanair.ie

Saudi Arabian Airlines Corp
(Saudia)
www.saudiairlines.com

Scandinavian Airline System (SAS)
www.sas.se

Singapore Airlines Ltd
www.singaporeair.com.sg

South African Airways
www.flysaa.com

Southwest Airlines Co
www.southwest.com

Swiss International Air Lines
www.swiss.com

Thai Airways International Ltd
www.thaiairways.com

Tyrolean Airways Tiroler
Luftfahrt GmbH
www.tyrolean.at

United Airlines, Inc
www.ual.com

United Express/Atlantic Coast
Airlines
www.atlanticcoast.com

US Airways
www.usairways.com

Varig
www.varig.com

Virgin Atlantic Airways Ltd
www.virgin-atlantic.com

Virgin Blue Airlines Pty Ltd
www.virginblue.com.au

Yemenia Airways Corp
www.yemenia.com

# Index

*Page numbers in italics indicate the location of illustrations*

**A**

accessibility, *90-98*
  airports and, 95-96, 99
  Americans with Disabilities Act (ADA), 91, 93, 99
  complaints about, 94, 95
  coping with, 95
  crutches, 94
  elderly passengers and, 96, 97
  guide dogs, 95, 96, *95*
  lavatories and, 94, 97
  regulations regarding, 91, 93
  wheelchairs, 92, 93, 94, 95, *90-94*
Adria Airways, 137
Aer Lingus, 146, *88, 124, 125, 146*
  carpeting on, 123
  Premier Class, 27, 134
Aero Design Services, 166-167, *167*
Aeroflot Russian International Airlines, 151, *125, 151*
AeroMexico, *83*
Aerosud Interiors, 68-69
Airbus, 20, 24, 59, 119, 128, 143, *24, 172, 173, 176, 181, 182, 183*
  Airbus A320, 46, 159
  Airbus A380, 23, 97, 127, 181
Air Canada, 146, *50, 106*
  Classe Affaires, 72
  maintenance, 104, 106
  NutriCuisine programme, 73
*Aircraft Interiors* magazine, California, 89
Air Florida, 58, 145
Air France, *16, 28, 29, 54, 148, 152, 154, 156, 158, 164*
  Concorde. *See* Concorde
  L'Espace programme, 19
  meal service on, 29
  seats, 16
Air Kazakhstan, *55*
airline industry, 59. *See also* aviation
  current state of, 177, 184
  deregulation and, 177
  financial state of, 121, 177, 184
  future of, 177-184
Air New Zealand, 113
airports
  accessibility in, 95-96, 99
  service in, 24
Air Tanzania, *50*
aisle carts. *See* meal service: trolleys
Alaska Airlines, 134, 164, *164, 165*
Alg, Vern, 93, 94, 95-96
Alitalia, 27, 146
all-one-class service. *See* one-class service

All Nippon Airways (ANA), 29, 89, 118, 132, *29, 82, 107*
amenity kits. *See* touchpoints: amenity kits
American Airlines, 132, *90, 95*
  Boeing B777, 24-25, 38, 49
  economy class, 49
  Flagship Suite, 21, 24-25
  More Room Throughout Coach project, 45-46
American Trans Air, *129*
Americans with Disabilities Act (ADA). *See* accessibility: ADA
Amies, Hardy, 153
Asiana Airlines, 21
Association of European Airlines, 93
Austrian Airlines, 27, *84*
Avianca Airlines, *82*
aviation. *See also* airline industry
  history of, 5-9

**B**

baggage stowage compartments. *See* overhead stowage bins
Balmain, Pierre, 148
Baron, Daniel, 89
bars, on-board, 30, 114, *29, 30, 31, 67, 114, 164*
bathrooms. *See* lavatories
beauty salon, 30, *30, 138*
Berg, Peter Christoph, 172
Bermack, Barbara, 24, 38, 49, 162-163
blue. *See* colour: blue
boarding-gate meal bags. *See* meal service: boarding-gate bags
Bock, Thomas, 20, *24*
Boeing Company, the, 59, *97, 159*
  Boeing B717, 66, 97
  Boeing B737, 49
  Boeing B737-200, 149
  Boeing B747
    crew rest facilities on, 165
    first class on, 16, 19, 125
    staircase carpeting on, 127
    upper deck of, 23, 29
  Boeing B747-400, 45, 68-69
  Boeing B777, 24-25, 38, 49, 125
  Boeing Business Jet (BBJ), 178-180
  Boeing Sonic Cruiser, 158, *159*
Bogash, Richard R., *82*
Boland, Michael M., 24, 38, 49
Bombardier Regional Jet, 45, 46-47, *45*
Boyd, James, 86-87
branding. *See* corporate branding programmes

Braniff International, 145, 150, *142, 143, 144, 145*
  corporate branding programme of, 58-59
Bregman, Bob, 75
British Aerospace BAe146, 121
British Airways, 96, 125, 132, 153, *16, 17, 25, 33, 34, 39, 43, 44, 56, 57, 65, 95, 96, 152, 155, 157, 160, 161*
  business class, 32-34
  corporate branding programme of, 56-57, 58, *56-57*
  Club World, 32-34, *34, 39*
  Concorde. *See* Concorde
  first class, 15-21
  meal service, 74-75
  sleeper seats, 16-17, 19, 24, 64, *17, 25*
  World Traveller Plus, 44, 45, 49, *44*
  Worldwide Art programme, 16, 19, *16*
British Caledonian, 148
Brown, Robert S., 69
Bruce Industries, 65
Brymon Airways, 96
Buck, Wendy, 66-67
bulkhead-mounted literature pockets. *See* literature pockets
bulkheads. *See* cabin dividers
bull-nosing, 124, 127-128, *124*
bunk beds, 22, 23, *22, 23*
business class, *26-39. See also* two-class service; one-class service
  business/first class, 38
  evolution of, 27
  fares for, 27, 32, 36, 38
  leather in, 134
  Lufthansa and PrivatAir service, 178-180
  meal service in, 28, 36, 75
  Qantas international business class, 170
  seats in, 27-34
  short-haul service and, 36
business travellers
  and corporate cutbacks, 44, 49
  future for, 180
  in business class, 36, 38
  in economy class, 46, 47
  on Concorde, 161-163
business work stations, 29, *29*
BWIA International Airways, 58, *50*

**C**

cabin dividers, 36, 44, 106, 107, 115, *105, 107, 162, 166*
Calder, Alexander, 145

carpeting, *122-129*
  colours of, 126
  installation of, 123, 127
  maintenance of, 109, 126, 128
  nicknames for, 128
  on staircases, 124, 127-128
  regulations concerning, 123, 125
  replacement of, 126
  wool vs. nylon, 123, 125-126
Cathay Pacific Airways, 89, 146, *50, 87*
change-outs, 47-49, 104, 116, 117, 126
children and infants, 97
China Southern Airlines, 85, *55, 73, 75, 78, 79, 86, 147*
Chown, Ford, 104, 108
cleaning. *See* maintenance
cleaning logs. *See* maintenance: problem-tracking systems
coach class. *See* economy class
colour, 36, *142-151*
  blue, 146-148, 149, 150
  cultural implications of, 143, 146-147
  emotional response to, 148, 149
  signage and, 150
  technology and, 150
  upgrades and, 167
Computergraphics ACA, 172, *front cover, 119, 172, 173, 174*
Concorde, *152-163*
  Air France, 154, 156-158, 163
  British Airways, 147, 155, 156, 159, 162, 163
  cabins of, 153, 155, 156
  decor of, 47, 155-158, 159, 163
  end of service of, 163
  fares for, 155, 162
  flying time of, 153, 162
  meal service on, 155, 158, *155, 158*
  seats for, 137, 153, 156, 159, 163
  space in, 153, 156
  stretching of, 154
  windows of, 154, *154*
Conran, Sir Terence, 159
Continental Airlines, 55, 58, 71, *26, 27, 28, 32, 37, 54, 64, 84, 93, 94, 112*
  accessibility considerations at, 93, 94, 95-96
  Business First, 27
Continental Express, 137, *118*
Cooper, Mike, 149
Cornman, Diane, 158
corporate branding programmes (CBPs), *50-59*
  and aircraft interiors, 56

brand loyalty, 58
differentiation of airlines
through, 59
examples of, 56-57, 58-59
goals for, 51-53, 58, 59
implementing, 53
running of, 58
setting up of, 53
crew-rest facilities, 165
Crossair, 137
curtains, 104
cutlery. *See* meal service: tableware

**D**

decals, use of, 50, 75, *50*
Deignan, David, 113, 128
Delta Air Lines, 132, 148, 151, *28,*
*69, 84, 87, 95, 151*
Business Elite, 28-29, 64, 134
menu of, 73
Delta Shuttle, 137
design concerns
accessibility and, 97, 99
carpeting and, 123, 128
colour and, 143, 145, 149
computer graphics and, 170-172
durability and, 114, 115, 118-
121, 175
examples of, 24-25, 38, 49
for exteriors, 16, 19, 56, 59
for interiors, 56, 59, 150, 167, 175
lighting and, 65-67, 68-69
maintenance and, 104, 113
dining. *See* meal service
disabled passengers. *See* accessibility
Douglass Interior Products, 139,
*130*
Draper, Gerry, 153, 154-155
drapes, 104
Ducasse, Alain, 158
Duenhaupt, Aage, 178, 180
durability, *114-120. See also* maintenance
and suppliers, 115, 116
surface treatments and, 119,
*119, 120*
testing for, 116, 118, 175
weight savings and, 115, 118-
119, 121, 126, 139

**E**

Eastern Airlines, 124, 128, 132,
145, *55, 124, 132, 166*
easyJet Airline Company, 177, *149*
orange colour of, 149
economy class, *40-48*
business travellers in, 44, 46, 49
decor in, 46, 47-49
discomfort in, 41
fares for, 41, 45
improvements in, 42, 45
meal service in, 41, 42, 71, 75, 77
seating configuration in, 44, *43*

seats in, 41-42, 45-46, 47-49
El Al Israel Airlines, *55*
Emirates Airline, 118, *12, 13, 58,*
*74, 75, 137*
Enterprise IG Japan, 163, 175
executive class. *See* business
class

**F**

FAA (Federal Aviation
Administration), 59, 123, 150,
166-167
FAR (Federal Aviation Regulation),
123, 125
fabric. *See* textiles
Factory, 159
Ferrara, Ryan, 116
first class, *12-25*
developments in, 13
fares for, 13, 23
leather in, 132
meal service in, 19, 71-72, 75-77
seats in, 13-15, 16-25, 170
flammability. *See* safety: flammability requirements
flight attendants
accessibility and, 93, 94
lighting and, 67
maintenance and durability and,
104, 113, 120, 121
meal service and, 71, 72
uniforms of, 147, 148, 153, 158
floor coverings (non-textile), 109,
*109*
food-and-beverage service. *See*
meal service
footrests. *See* seats: legrests

**G**

Gargano, Edward L., 75
George Design Studio, 58-59,
150, *14, 36, 42, 43, 83, 142, 143,*
*144, 145*
George, Philip, 58-59, 131, 145,
150
Girard, Alexander, 145
Golden Falcon Fleet (Eastern
Airlines), 145
gooseneck reading lights. *See*
lighting: gooseneck reading lights
grab bars. *See* handrails and grab
bars
Gulf Air, 132, *50*

**H**

handicapped passengers. *See*
accessibility
handrails and grab bars, 94, 97
illuminated, 66, *97*
Hawaiian Airlines, 124, 128, *54,*
*124*
Henry, Susan, 77, 113, 128, 175
Hooper, Stan, 145
Hoover Industries, 121, 139, 175
hygiene. *See* maintenance

**I**

Iberia Airlines of Spain, 151, *14,*
*55, 70, 72, 151*
Ilyushin IL-86, 127
Indian Airlines, *151*
Infante, Marisa, 121, 139, 175
International Air Transport
Association (IATA), 44, 177
Internet and email, 86-87
in-flight literature pockets. *See* lit-
erature pockets

**J**

Jack Tinker Agency, 58
Jaffe, Steve, 65
Japan Airlines (JAL), 103, *21, 59,*
*76, 93, 169, 170, 171*
first class, 21
meal service of, 75-77, *76*
Skysleeper Solo, 170
Jet Airways, *50*
jetBlue Airways, *55*
colour blue and, 147
decor scheme of, 46, 137, 159
success of, 49, 177
Jullies, Owen Graham, 77
Junkin Safety Appliance
Company, *92*

**K**

KLM Royal Dutch Airlines, 27, 85,
*84, 92*
Korean Air, *80*

**L**

Lacroix, Christian, 158
LanChile, *50*
Landor Associates, 156
Lantal Textiles, 137, 143, 149,
*front cover, 106, 134*
LaSusa, Patrice, 118-119
lavatories, *109, 120, 166, 173, 181*
accessibility in, 94, 97
lighting in, 65
maintenance of, 109, 113
touchpoints in, 79, 89
Lawrence, Harding, 58, 145
leather, 59, 159, *130-138*
care of, 118, 137
durability of, 131
in business class, 134
in first class, 132
in one-class aircraft, 137
natural variations in, 139
synthetic, 118-119, 131, 134
legrests. *See* seats: legrests
lighting, *62-69*
and accessibility, 97
changes in, 63-64, 69
gooseneck reading lights, 16,
29, 64-65, *64-66*
'mood lighting', 30, 65-67, 68-
69, *66*
new uses of, 65-67
Lindbergh, Charles, 130, *130*

literature pockets, 42, 71, 111,
112, *105, 111, 112, 137, 162*
long thin routes, 177-178
Loschiavo, L.J. Jr. (Larry Lo), 125,
127
Lovegrove, Ross, 170
Ludlum, Kenneth V., 127-128
Ludlum Products Company, 127-
128, *124*
Luethi, Monika, 137
Lufthansa German Airlines, 103,
177, *18, 53, 55, 178, 179, 180*
and PrivatAir, 178-180
first class, 18, 20
Lufthansa Technik, 178, 180

**M**

maintenance, *102-112. See also*
durability
at downline stations, 113
carpets and, 106, 109, 126
colour and, 143
effects of smoking and, 103, 121
fabrics and leather and, 104,
106, 107, 137
in galleys, 109
in lavatories, 109, 113
literature pockets and, 111
new standards for, 103
problem-tracking systems, 104
surface treatments and, 105,
106, *105, 107*
mandatory certification testing.
*See* safety
Maritz Travel Company, 24, 38, 49
marketing campaigns, 75
Markham, Beryl, 130, *130*
Martin-Vegue, Phyllis, 24-25
McDonnell Douglas DC8, 145
McDonnell Douglas DC10, 59
meal service, *70-77, 114, 148, 155*
boarding-gate bags, 75
cutbacks in, 71
gourmet-style, 71, 72, 75-77
healthy food, 72-73
hygiene standards, 74
in business class, 29, 36, 75
in economy class, 41, 42, 71,
75, 77
in first class, 71, 75
new trends in, 71-72
on-board chefs, 72
on long-haul services, 75-77
presentation, 71, 73-75, 77
tableware, 73-75, 89
trolleys, 19, 71, 109, *109*
wines and spirits, 77
medical concerns, 97
Medline Industries, *92*
Mercury International Travel, 24,
38, 49, 162
Meridiana, 77, 113, 121, 128, *54*
Mesa Airlines, 137
Mexicana Airlines, 54, *54, 77,*
*122, 123, 129, 151*

MGR Foamtex, 116, *116, 117*
MHM North America, 75
Middle East Airlines (MEA), 54, 134, *54, 93, 134*
Minor Miscellaneous Items (MMIs). *See* touchpoints: Minor Miscellaneous Items
Mohawk Industries, 123, 128, *107, 124, 126, 127*
Moris, Lamberto G., 38, 49
music, 85

**N**
National Airlines, 145, *87*
Northwest Airlines, 27, 77, 113, 128, 175, *50, 87*

**O**
Ogawa, Alan J., 75-77
one-class service, 137, 139, 178-180
oneworld alliance, 51
overhead stowage bins, 66, 108, 120, 121, 153, *108, 157*

**P**
Palacio, Loyola de, 93
Pan American World Airways, 13, 58, 59, *14, 36, 42, 43, 50, 83*
  Clipper Class, 36, 131
  'dining in the sky', 59, 71
passenger control pad, 29, 63-64, 65, *69, 136*
Peterson, Steve V., 139
Pham, Alina, 167
Philippine Airlines, *22, 23, 50*
  bunk beds, 22, 23, *22, 23*
placards. *See* signage
'pod' seats. *See* seats: sleeper seats: 'pod' style
PrivatAir, 125, 137, 147, *178, 179, 180*
  and Lufthansa, 178-180
public address systems, 85
Pucci, Emilio, 145
Putman, Andrée, 156

**Q**
Qantas Airways, 118, *15, 20, 40, 54, 80, 81, 83, 85, 110*
  business-class refurbishment, 170
  first class, 20, 21
Qualiflyer Group, 51

**R**
Raia, Jack, 115-116
Rathmanner, Bill, 166-167
refurbishment. *See* upgrades
Regional Jet. *See* Bombardier Regional Jet
reconfiguration of interiors, 170
regulatory requirements, 111, 150, 166
  carpeting and, 123, 125
  in corporate branding

programmes, 53, 56
  maintenance and, 108
rest rooms. *See* lavatories
Rose, Jon, 116
Ruffolo, Jeff, 85
Ryanair, 75, 177

**S**
safety
  and MMIs, 79
  flammability requirements
    carpeting and, 123, 125
    in upgrades, 166, 167
    new products and, 116, 118
  lighting and, 68
  safety cards, 111
  safety signs, 108
  structural certification requirements, 166-167
  testing and, 116, 125
Sandiford, David, 123, 128
Saudi Arabian Airlines (Saudia), 58, *50*
Scandinavian Airline System (SAS), 27, 89, 103, 175, *36, 48, 59, 88, 114, 115*
  EuroClass, 36
scents, 109
Schneller, Inc., 116, *109*
seat-back pockets. *See* literature pockets
seats
  armrests, 64, 94, 120, *94*
  blue, *147, 151*
  certification standards, 166-167
  convertible, 36
  covers for, 116-118, 121, 139, 175
  damage to, 120, 121
  Eames 'Chair-in-the-Air', 20, 23, 132, *20, 21, 119*
  for business class, 27, 28-29, 30-38, *26-39*
  for economy class, 41-42, 45-46, 47-49, *40-48*
  headrest covers, 47, 111, 117, 121, 137, *111, 154, 156*
  legrests, 13, 14, 28, 29, *14, 28, 106*
  maintenance and durability of, 111, 143, 175
  seat pitch, 27-28, 41-42, 44, 45, 111
  sleeper seats, *12, 14-26, 28, 34, 35, 37, 39, 171, 183*
    in business class, 27, 32-34
    in first class, 16-25, 170
    lighting and, 64
    meal service and, 71
    'pod' style, 16, 17, 19
    spread of 'pod' style, 21, 23
  slimline, 42, 111
  swivel, 20, 25
security procedures, new, 73, 113, 180
SER-MAT, 125, 127, *124*

Sheahan & Associates, 59, 89
Sheahan, Peter, 59, 89
signage, 95, 108, 109, *108, 109*
  colours for, 150
Sim, Stan, 68-69
Singapore Airlines, *35, 48, 55, 133, 151*
  first class, 20, 118, 132
  flight attendants' uniform, 148
  maintenance and, 103
  Raffles Class, 34
  seats, 34, 151
  touchpoints and, 86-87
Sky Marketing Services, 82
SkyTeam, 51, 83
SMWM, 24-25, 38, 49
South African Airways, 113, 151, 165, *52, 81, 86, 151*
  carpeting on, 125, 128
  corporate branding programme of, 56
  first class, 23, 64
  meal service on, 77
  Millennium Interior programme, 56
Southwest Airlines, 145, 177, *126, 127*
  carpeting on, 126-127, 128
  corporate branding programme of, 58
  economy class, 49
staircases, 124, 127-128, *181, 183*
Star Alliance, 51, *51*
Stein, Richard, 163, 175
Swiss International Air Lines, 23, 132
Swissair, 64, 119, 172, *20*
  Eames 'Chair-in-the-Air', 20, 23, 132, *20, 21, 119*
SYAIR Designs, 69

**T**
Tapis Corporation, 118-119, *118*
Tecmath of North America, 99, 150
textiles. *See also* leather
  maintenance and durability of, 118, 175
  synthetic, 118-119
Thai Airways International, 21, 148, *54, 148*
  on-board souvenirs, 89
Timco Engineered Systems, 115
toilets. *See* lavatories
Toomey Design Group, 150
Toomey, Michael Clark, 150
touchpoints, *78-88*
  amenity kits, 82, 84, 89, *88*
  branding and, 80
  coordination of, 86
  importance of, 80-81
  Minor Miscellaneous Items (MMIs), 79-85, 168
  playing cards, *87*
  sample boxes, 82
tourist class. *See* economy class

Trident 2, 34
trolleys. *See* meal service: trolleys
TWA, 13, 28, *28, 129*
two-class service, 20, 27-28, 30-32, 38, 134
Tyrolean Airways, 137

**U**
U-Land Airlines, 134, *118*
uniforms, 49, 147-148, 153, 158
United Airlines, 118, 132, 165, 167, *19, 37, 47, 48, 58, 80, 82, 87, 96, 102, 103, 108, 110, 129*
  business class, 64
  first class, 19, 21, 64
  United Economy Plus Class, 45
United Express/Atlantic Coast Airlines, 63, *45, 46*
  decor and identity of, 46-48
upgrades, *164-174*
  categories of, 166, 168
  computer graphics and, 170-172
  cost of, 166, 168
  examples of, 170, 175
  launching of, 168, 172
  new product testing in, 166, 167, 175
  planning of, 167-168, 170, 175
  regulatory requirements and, 166
US Airways, 134, *107, 129*

**V**
van der Meulen, Peter A., 99, 150
Varig, *50*
Varley, John, 77, 113, 121, 128
Virgin Atlantic Airways, 58, 59, 147, 148, 177, *30, 31, 62, 63, 67, 135, 136, 138, 147*
  beauty salon, 30, *30, 138*
  lighting system, 64, 66-67
  meal service, 71
  Premium Economy Class, 45, 49
  Upper Class, 30, 64, 66-67, 71, 89, 134
Virgin Blue, 147

**W**
Webster, Ray, 149
Weiner, David, 99, 121
Wells, Mary, 58, 145
WESSCO International, 75
Western Pacific Airlines, 145
wetlease agreement: example of, 178-180
wheelchairs. *See* accessibility: wheelchairs
Wright, Orville and Wilbur, 5-9, 184, *4, 6, 8, 9, 176, 184*

**Y**
Yemenia Airways, 128, *151*